W9-BYZ-607

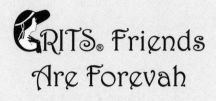

GRITS® Friends
Are Forevah

BY DEBORAH FORD

The Grits® (Girls Raised in the South) Guide to Life

Puttin' on the GRITS™

GRITS® Friends Are Forevah

A SOUTHERN-STYLE CELEBRATION OF WOMEN

Deborah Ford

DUTTON

To my sisters, Virginia, Barbara, and Mavis. My life would not be complete without you, and you've always been there for me. You've been best friends, companions, and, of course, partners in crime.

DUTTON
Published by Penguin Group (USA) Inc.
375 Hudson Street, New York, New York 10014, U.S.A.
Penguin Group (Canada), 90 Eglinton Avenue East, Suite 700, Toronto, Ontario M4P
2Y3, Canada (a division of Pearson Penguin Canada Inc.); Penguin Books Ltd, 80
Strand, London WC2R 0RL, England; Penguin Ireland, 25 St Stephen's Green, Dublin
2, Ireland (a division of Penguin Books Ltd); Penguin Group (Australia), 250
Camberwell Road, Camberwell, Victoria 3124, Australia (a division of Pearson Australia
Group Pty Ltd); Penguin Books India Pvt Ltd, 11 Community Centre, Panchsheel Park,
New Delhi - 110 017, India; Penguin Group (NZ), cnr Airborne and Rosedale Roads,
Albany, Auckland 1310, New Zealand (a division of Pearson New Zealand Ltd); Penguin
Books (South Africa) (Pty) Ltd, 24 Sturdee Avenue, Rosebank, Johannesburg 2196,
South Africa

Penguin Books Ltd, Registered Offices: 80 Strand, London WC2R 0RL, England

Published by Dutton, a member of Penguin Group (USA) Inc.

First printing, January 2006
10 9 8 7 6 5 4 3 2 1

Copyright © Grits, Inc., 2005
All rights reserved

GRITS IS A REGISTERED TRADEMARK OF GRITS, INC. REGISTERED TRADEMARK—
MARCA REGISTRADA

LIBRARY OF CONGRESS CATALOGING-IN-PUBLICATION DATA
has been applied for.

ISBN 0-525-94918-6

Printed in the United States of America
Set in Adobe Garamond
Designed by Daniel Lagin

Without limiting the rights under copyright reserved above, no part of this publication may be reproduced, stored in or introduced into a retrieval system, or transmitted, in any form, or by any means (electronic, mechanical, photocopying, recording, or otherwise), without the prior written permission of both the copyright owner and the above publisher of this book.

The scanning, uploading, and distribution of this book via the Internet or via any other means without the permission of the publisher is illegal and punishable by law. Please purchase only authorized electronic editions, and do not participate in or encourage electronic piracy of copyrighted materials. Your support of the author's rights is appreciated.

Contents

Introduction:
Growing a Friendship Tree

If you drive through the Deep South, you can't miss the massive, majestic old trees known as live oaks, spreading their branches in the town squares and over the gracious mansions and mansionettes. The live oak stands tall and proud, its trunk broad and sturdy, its limbs providing shade even on the hottest Southern summer day. When I see these trees, I think of the settler who set them down years ago, hoping that one day his children or grandchildren could take a bit of rest beneath their leaves. He knew he wouldn't be around to watch them enjoy them in their full glory, but he wanted to share with those who came after him. Honey, I wish I had the time to set myself down in that shade, drink a cool glass of sweet tea, and thank him for the favor.

GRITS GLOSSARY

Live oak [liv ok] n. *A species of oak tree referred to as "live" because its leaves remain green throughout the year, just like Southern ladies, who are green and fresh throughout their lives. These massive trees grow to great heights and widths and are long-lived; the famous live oak of Waycross, Georgia, has stood for at least three centuries.*

We Southerners are a bit like the trees that make our landscape so beautiful. Though different in many ways, each is crowned with beautiful leaves. The leaves shade, shield, and soften our lives. They add fullness, depth, and color to the seasons of our lives. Whenever I think of these leaves, I think of friends. Every season brings change, and every friend grows and changes with each day and season of her life. If a pesky neighbor sometimes seems more like Spanish moss than a beautiful leaf, that's fine, too; those low-hanging parasites often make the grand old trees even more beautiful to behold.

PEARL OF WISDOM

When she sang "winter, spring, summer, or fall, all you've got to do is call," Carole King must have been talking about GRITS!

People often plant trees in remembrance of loved ones who have passed. That's a beautiful tradition, and I can't think of anyone who wouldn't be proud to see a graceful magnolia or strong oak planted in her memory. But there's no reason that we can't plant a tree in honor of our favorite GRITS who are still alive. Do you have a friend who's helped you plan your wedding or gotten you through a divorce? Who's helped you lose those last ten pounds or brought you butter pecan ice cream to help you gain them? Who's held your hand through labor pains or babysat when your kids are just pains in the neck? Let that wonderful GRITS friend know that you care by planting a tree in her honor. Plant it in her yard—though be sure to get her permission before you start digging up her lawn!—or plant trees in your own yard as part of your own friendship garden. She'll be honored, your yard will look better, and your teenage daughter who's

Ten Reasons Southern Women
Are Strong as Oaks and Beautiful
as Georgia Peaches

1. *We may look beautiful and graceful, but we've got big old strong roots to protect us against all kinds of weather.*
2. *Those autumn-leaf peepers just can't get enough of us; they know we're even better as we mature.*
3. *We love to nurture—children, neighbors, friends, and even the occasional cat shelter in our branches. And sometimes we even give tired old men the thrill of our shade.*
4. *We make everything around us look better without even trying.*
5. *We love our land and hold on tightly to even the sandiest soil.*
6. *We require regular maintenance—a trim to keep that beautiful shape, some nourishment when we're looking peaked—but we're worth all the attention.*
7. *We may add a new ring every year, but that extra padding just makes us look more majestic.*
8. *We don't mind dabbing on the color to put on a fabulous show.*
9. *We may get a little craggy with age, but that's what we call character, sugar.*
10. *There's a lifetime of memories in everything from our bark (yes, we get angry, too) to our buds.*

always yelling at you about recycling will think her mom's a hero for helping the environment.

When you buy your tree, make sure that you ask the people at the nursery how to plant and care for it; plants need love and attention just like us beautiful Southern women. Whatever you do, don't forget to water it in the following weeks. Nobody is going to feel honored by a dried-up old stick!

If you treasure your friends as much as most Southern women, you may end up with a regular friendship forest. Sit down with your Southern girlfriends on hot summer days and think of the friendships you have to thank for the beautiful shade.

SECTION I

The Birth of Friendship

"The person who tries to live alone will not succeed as a human being. His heart withers if he does not answer another heart. His mind shrinks away if he hears only the echoes of his own thoughts and finds no other inspiration."—PEARL S. BUCK

CHAPTER 1

The Seed of Friendship

"Make new friends, but keep the old, one is silver and the other's gold." —GIRL SCOUT SONG

"Walking with a friend in the dark is better than walking alone in the light." —HELEN KELLER, ALABAMA

I remember the days when locking your doors was unheard-of here in the South. Up North, people had bars on their windows and bars on their hearts, but down here, doors were always opened to family and friends. When the hot weather came, we'd sleep with the doors wide open, nothing between us and the outside but a flimsy little screen and, believe me, we never worried about anything breaking in, except maybe a few mosquitoes. In fact, in parts of the South, houses even had "sleeping porches" for those nights when the air was so hot and thick you felt you could swim through it, and families (and sometimes whole neighborhoods) would take in the cool night breezes together, unafraid of anything but the chirping of the tree frogs and crickets disturbing their rest. Family and friends could walk right into our homes any time they wanted, and they were always welcome, even that cousin who never seemed to find a job but could always find the door at supper time.

These days, even in parts of the South, we close the latch, the dead bolt, and the bars securely at night. We worry about stopping to help the stranded motorist by the side of the road in case he might be a criminal. We worry about people who just want to say a kind word to our beautiful children, in case they might be child snatchers. There's so much worry that we sometimes forget to show basic kindness.

Though the reasons for our fears may be sound, it's a pity that the doors are shut, windows are locked, and hearts are closed up tight.

In these times, it's more important than ever that we turn to our friends. GRITS we can love and trust are still out there, and they want us to reach out in friendship as much as we want them to come to us. Friendship can throw open the doors and cure us of those fears. When we know our neighbors, when we know we have someone to turn to, we'll be able to sleep as tightly as we did in the old days. We have to actually plant the seed of friendship if we ever want it to grow. Go on over and say hello; you'll be glad you did.

GRITS GLOSSARY

Girlfriend [gərl frend] n. *1. Your best and most crucial friend. She's the truest, closest, and most beloved woman you know. In other words, she "gets it," whatever it is you need for her to "get." From the most minute details to the big picture, your true friend makes your experiences more real! 2. Your forevah friend!*

Add a Pearl, Drop a Pearl

While every Southern woman worth the name has a strand, or more, of pearls, every Southern woman's pearls are a little bit different. Some are long and showy, some short and simple, and some dramatic multiple strands. Some are hand-harvested, and some have never met an oyster, no matter what that loud woman at the country club claims.

We Southern women change day to day, a fact Southern men

won't ever let us forget, sugah, and we love to have our jewelry change with us. That's why true Southern women love add a pearl, drop a pearl necklaces. We can wear just a few pearls on a simple chain if we're feeling delicate and demure or, if we're feeling the need to be glamorous, we can add charms and jewels.

We Southern women would never add and drop our friends as quickly as we drop our pearls; we're too fiercely loyal and loving for that. Women in other parts of the country may go through their friends like paper tissues, but GRITS are fine, embroidered handkerchiefs to be valued. When our friends must leave our lives, they stay in our hearts.

We do, however, change the way we approach and deepen our friendships throughout our lives. We add some pearls of wisdom, and we drop others.

I'm glad to share with you some of the "pearls" that I apply to friendship. I don't pretend to know everything, or even most things, about friendship. If I did, I wouldn't be a very fun friend to be around. In fact, every day I learn a bit more, and I realize how much I've grown and changed over my life. Still, there are some Southern truths about friendship. Some might apply to your life, and some might not, so you can add or drop the pearls as you like to make a necklace of your friendships that you can wear proudly.

Add a Pearl, Drop a Pearl

Adding New Pearls to the Strand

- *My mother always taught me that no one is better than I am, nor am I better than anyone else. Keep an open mind when meeting new people, and don't snub anyone because of first* appearances. If you don't judge her before you know her, you may find that the woman with the bad attitude, frizzy hair, and moth-eaten coat could be your new best friend.

- We Southern women don't want to burden people with our problems, so sometimes when we're feeling lonely, we're liable to sit around by ourselves. But that's not going to help anyone. The best way to forget your troubles and loneliness is to reach out and help others, so shake those little legs and get moving! Volunteer at a nursing home, a hospital, the hunting lodge the day after deer season ends, or anywhere there might be people in need of comfort. Reach out to others in need, and you'll find that your own loneliness melts away.

- Birds of a feather flock together, and they don't argue about how to decorate the nest. Think about what moves you, whether it's spirituality, knitting, or even skydiving, and find groups or clubs that share your interests. Even if you don't meet close friends, you'll have fun, and your group will always have something to talk about.

- If you're lonely, chances are someone else around you is, too. Reach out to that quiet woman at the office, the neighbor who no one on the street seems to know, or the lady who always sits by herself in the rear pew at church. Say hello, and you might discover a pretty little GRITS smile hidden under that shyness.

- And my goodness, darling, never leave the house without looking presentable, since you never know when you're going to meet someone new. No GRITS worth her mother's china would ever be seen outside of the house without being ready to face the world.

Everybody knows that Southern girls make the best friends. GRITS treasure their friends the way they treasure their family heirlooms, and they don't mind the tarnish because they know there's silver underneath. I don't know where I'd be without my friends' listening ears, advice, laughter, strength, unconditional love, and just plain being there. A true GRITS friend makes your victories sweeter, your laughter longer, and your pain gentler. A Southern lady won't praise herself, but her GRITS girlfriend will praise her to the skies. She'll stand by your side through nights of crying and long hours at the beauty parlor. She might know your true hair color, but she isn't talking.

GRITS NEED ALL KINDS OF FRIENDS!

Once-a-Year Friends: *You don't see them often, but when you do, it's firecrackers.*

How-Y'all-Doing Friends: *More than strangers, and less than deep friends. GRITS meet a couple dozen how y'all doing friends everywhere they go, so your man can just hold his horses and wait.*

Best Friends: *Always ready to share laughter or pain.*

Hair-Dye Friends: *The only people you really, really trust.*

GRITS love to have things in common with their friends, but they know that it's more important to have shared values than shared interests. GRITS need to believe in the same things, such as loyalty, family, pride, and heritage, and they don't mind so much if you have bad taste in movies, pies, or men. Tastes can change, but the things that matter stay the same. With a GRITS by your side, you can survive anything from leg warmers to line dancing with grace and style.

Southern Girls Go Together Like:

Shrimp and Grits
Whiskey and Branch
Biscuits and Gravy
Wine and Whine
Trucks and Mudflaps
Men and Dawgs
Milk and Cornbread
Children and Kisses
Peas and Carrots (Forrest Gump was right, sugah!)

When you choose a GRITS for a friend, you never have to be afraid that you're imposing. GRITS don't mind if you call in the middle of the night; in fact, they'd be upset to know you were in trouble and didn't call. When you choose a Southern girl as a friend, you're choosing someone who's loyal. She'll stay with you through bad times, and she won't get jealous in the good times. True GRITS aren't fair- or foul-weather, but all-weather friends. GRITS will never mind hearing from you, honey, they'll just kindly require that you spill all the juicy details!

PEARL OF WISDOM

"She didn't care what kind of mess you were, or what people were saying about you, or where your record was on the charts—she just saw another yearning soul standing there asking for love, whether you knew you were asking for it or not and, by God, she was going to see that you got it."—Rosanne Cash, on Minnie Pearl, both Tennessee GRITS

GRITS GLOSSARY

Fair-Weather Friend [fer we-thər frend] n. *A friend who wants to share only the good times. She'll play bridge at the country club, take you shopping to the finest stores, and flirt with the best-looking men, but when the bills come due and the men have traded you in for a younger model, she's nowhere to be found.*

Foul-Weather Friend [faul we-thər frend] *A friend who loves commiserating with you, but resents your good fortune. She'll cry with you over your dingy trailer and botched dye job, but the minute you win the lottery, she's on to some other hard-luck case.*

GRITS Know They Can Ring a Belle for Any Occasion

Bar Belles: *Attorney friends, workout partners, or drinking buddies.*
Wedding Belles: *Women who've been a bridesmaid more than four times.*
School Belles: *School friends, teachers, students (of any age), or mothers you meet at the PTA.*

Christmas Belles: *Friends you see only on the holidays.*

Crystal Belles: *Your high-falutin' friends from Junior League or the country club.*

Dinner Belles: *That wonder-cook who's the star of every potluck and progressive dinner.*

Church Belles: *Bible study, choir, or Sunday School friends.*

Cow Belles: *University of Southern Mississippi Coeds. Farm girls as well.*

Dumb Belles: *GRITS who don't listen to their mothers!*

Wanna-Be Belles: *Newcomers. Bless your hearts, we're happy to have you here!*

The Buddy System

Even as little girls, or Instant GRITS as I like to call them, Southerners go out of their way to meet people, and that need to make friends continues even as we blossom into womanhood. Being a friend is a role that we Southerners cherish. Our mothers know that children need to be trained in the art of being a friend, and most of them teach us by example.

When I was a child, making friends was easy for little Instant GRITS. I grew up on the Holt Road in Limestone County, Alabama. The twenty or so kids in the neighborhood were not only friends, but family. We worked, played, and went to school together. We may not all have been best friends in school, but we made sure we helped each other out, especially if someone dared to pick on one of us. We even wore each other's clothes.

After school and during the summer, we fished, looked

for snakes, rode horses, and played in the barn loft. If it snowed in the winter, we would put on our old rubber boots and slide (you couldn't call it skating!) on the frozen pond for hours. Nothing was better than the "snow cream" our mothers would make!

Imaginary Friends

Southern girls love to be near their friends. In fact, sometimes they love them so much that, when there isn't a real friend around, they have to make one up. My niece, Lauren, had an imaginary friend named Fancy Melissa. Lauren was the only girl in the family, and I guess she needed a female buddy to help her deal with her two older brothers, Zach and Tyler.

I used to keep Lauren quite a bit, and she, Fancy Melissa, and I had a grand old time. We dressed up, put on makeup, and spent hours making up new stories, especially about the Three Little Pigs, and the three of us were, of course, the little piglets.

Eventually Lauren started calling herself Fancy Melissa. Fancy Melissa's favorite outfit was her white rabbit-fur jacket and her white cowboy boots. Her chubby little cheeks were adorable, and she painted her little lips red. She topped it all off with her fabulous prissy attitude!

We loved Fancy so much that we decided to make her part of the family. When I developed a line of chenille clothing, each piece was named after a member of my family or a friend. The whitest and frilliest vest of all had to be named "Fancy Melissa."

—for my niece, Lauren "Fancy Melissa" Thornton
   Alabama

When I went to my hometown of Athens, Alabama, for a book signing last year, I was extremely touched that several of my elementary school friends came to see me. Kay, Vicki, and Donna were all there! More than forty years had passed, but it seemed like yesterday we were swinging on the swing set.

The girls, now ladies, who played softball with me through many summers were there, and even some of my teachers made it. Ms. Hamilton, our P.E. teacher, is the lady who taught me that we don't sweat, we glisten, and that girls can be both competitive and feminine. Ms. Hightower, my home economics teacher, emphasized the importance of doing the best you can with what you have. She always wore three-inch heels, even though she was six feet tall. Ms. Black, my history teacher, was always available to just talk. I can't forget Mrs. Holland, our sweet librarian, and Mrs. Usery, the English teacher who taught us to love our language. What better friends could a little girl have than her teachers? These wonderful ladies touched my heart, and I must confess it made my day, and maybe my year, to see these women.

Things are changing today; there are more latchkey kids, and neighbors are often strangers. For children who are alone much of the time, it can be harder to make friends, so it's even more important than ever to stay involved in our children's lives. I was a single mother, and I taught in the same junior high school my daughters attended. Both daughters played on my volleyball and softball teams. We may not have had dinner at home much, but we were together. In fact, I probably had dinner with my volleyball and softball players more than their parents did.

Teaching school wasn't very lucrative, but the time I spent with my children and their friends was invaluable. For some kids these days, school and home are separate, but they don't have to be. Just because we're holding full-time jobs doesn't mean that we can't be friends to our daughters—yes, even when they turn thirteen. But don't worry, they only think you're the most embarrassing woman on earth for about six years.

Schoolmates are our most precious friends outside of our own families, and parents and siblings can make those school days even better. Childhood is a time of learning and loafing, of games and girlfriends, of secrets and sharing, of cliques and clubs. And here in the South, it's also about family, community, and, of course, becoming a lady.

Some Folks Are More Athletic Than Others

I've known my best friend, Brenda, since we were four years old. Back then, we got into a lot of trouble together, but we always got out of it in the end. One summer, we decided that we needed to "get into shape," so we pulled out our old bicycles and headed off. I followed right behind Brenda. We circled into the new elementary school, and then Brenda pulled up onto the sidewalk with me right on her tail. Suddenly, CRASH! I hit the curb at full speed and went over my handlebars and right into a hedge. As I stood up, trying to recover my dignity, Brenda ran over to make sure that I was all right. I laughed and said that I had no idea what I'd done wrong. Brenda explained that you didn't just ride into the curb; you had to lift up your handlebars.

Years passed, and we married and moved away from each other. One day, Brenda called, saying that she'd be in town for the day, and she'd love for me to come to her sister's house after church. We drove to her sister's house in an unfamiliar area of town. I looked at the end of the block, and I started to squeal: "We're here! We're here! It's right down there."

Squinting, my husband asked how I could see the numbers all the way at the end of the street.

"Oh, I can't see the numbers at all, but I see Brenda: She just went flying through the air over the back of the carport."

We pulled into the driveway just as Brenda was climbing up the slight incline from the backyard. She had gone tail over teeth down the hill after misjudging the spring on her nephew's pogo stick.

—Sandra B. Speer
Georgia

Well-Seasoned GRITS

As we grow up, even we GRITS sometimes neglect to make new friends. We become content with our families and the GRITS who we've grown to know and love. We may be blessed with loving and supportive families, so we don't challenge ourselves to go out and meet new friends. We may have loving and treasured GRITS for girlfriends, so we think that we have enough. We may think that life goes too fast, and we're too busy, to take the time to meet new friends.

One of the secrets to making friends is to BYOB! No, I don't mean to carry a bottle around with you; I mean to Be Your Own Best friend. Treat yourself well by keeping your body and mind in shape through exercise, spirituality, and learning. Go out and explore your interests on your own, and learn to find something that you can do well and with pride. Take some time to treat yourself, whether it's a facial or a special piece of glimmering jewelry, and realize that you deserve it. If you can BYOB, you will feel better inside and out, and others will see and be attracted to what is good in you.

Whatever our excuses, and however content we may be with the way things are, we need to go out and meet new friends as we move through life. In today's world, with family spread far apart, with all the bad things we see every day, it's more important than ever that we share our lives with the people around us.

If you're too busy to make friends, honey, you're too busy for life. When you're ninety, are you going to be proud of your perfectly clean house, your job promotion, and your shiny new car, or are you going to be proud of all the wonderful women you've known in your life? As we grow up, we become well-seasoned GRITS, with just a little pat of butter here and there, and we're much better when we have some other tasty dishes by our sides.

PEARL OF WISDOM

*A true friend knows the song in your heart and sings it back to you
when you can't. I have a friend with whom I can share my innermost
thoughts and know that she can be trusted with them. Sharing will
lighten the burden, even if a solution is not found immediately. True
friendship is freedom.*

Throughout our lives, we play many roles, whether we're
children, students, workers, spouses, or parents, and as our
roles change, our need for friends changes, too. A young
woman on her first job needs other girls to complain about
the boss with. A young mother needs other women who
understand what it is like to have a pot burning on the stove
and a baby underfoot. A recently divorced woman needs
someone to hold her hand while she gets back on her feet. A
woman with her first grandchild needs someone who won't
be bored with all of her baby pictures. A widow needs to
share her grief with someone who has lost her own partner in
life. As important as it is to maintain our old friendships, we
also need to meet new women to match our new lives.

People tell me that as they grow into mature (I wouldn't
dare say "older" about a GRITS, sugah) women, making
friends seems harder. I think that we can make friends at all
stages in our lives, but like anything else, it takes a bit more
time and effort as we grow up.

Occasionally, when you meet a friend, you know that your
friendship was meant to be. I met my friend Carolyn on a
ladies tennis team. Carolyn and I could have known right
away that we'd hit it off; we were even wearing the exact

same tennis outfits. It seemed like whenever we attended a luncheon or party together, we'd show up wearing the same clothes, right down to our shoes. After a while, we took to calling each other before an event to make sure that we didn't look like the Bobbsey twins. Our similarities went a lot deeper than matching clothes; in fact, though I didn't know it at the time, we were both pregnant when we met. We gained the same amount of weight during our pregnancies, and her child and my second daughter were born on the same day. It turns out that we even had the same taste in men; Carolyn had dated my husband before I knew him.

More often, even we GRITS have to work to meet friends. The more you put yourself out in the world, whether it's getting a job after your children have moved out, volunteering in your spare afternoons, or joining a local bridge club, the more opportunities you'll have to meet other GRITS. The fact is, honey, you can't meet new friends by sitting at home watching *Dr. Phil* and doing your nails, though if you have the time, that sure does sound like fun.

Some People Just Click

Always keep your eyes open for potential GRITS girlfriends, because they can come into your life in the strangest ways. Oprah Winfrey met her close friend Gayle King in 1977. Back then, Oprah was an anchorwoman at WJZ-TV in Baltimore, and Gayle was working her way up through the ranks as a production assistant. Although Gayle was low in the station pecking order, and Gayle hardly knew her, Oprah reached out to her on the night of a bad snowstorm. She offered to let Gayle stay at her place for the night, and even offered her clothes to wear. The two women stayed up all night talking. In an interview with Lillian Ross of the New Yorker, *Gayle said of Oprah: "Some people just click. We clicked. We haven't stopped talking since. Oprah knows all the dirt. We never run out of things to talk about. We have so many things in common. Our shoe size is the same, ten. Our contact lenses have the same prescription. Our phone numbers—it just happened—are the same, but backward."*

Once you meet new acquaintances, you have to be available to them so that friendships can grow. If a woman asks you to lunch or to join her reading group, and you turn her down, she might not ask again. Being out and being available are the keys to making acquaintances, and from those acquaintances, friendships are born. Yes, it's harder as you go through life, but it isn't impossible if you put in the time and the effort, and always keep your GRITS smile on your beautiful face. So get up, dust yourself off, and go out and meet some new GRITS girlfriends.

Lipstick Sisters

Sometimes, you recognize a GRITS who can be your friend at a glance. The memory of it is as fresh as if it had happened today. I was walking down the street when I passed a young woman of maybe twenty-five. Our eyes instantly locked as we recognized a "red lipstick sister." Her makeup was artfully applied, but what really stood out were her perfectly shaped and very full red lips. She smiled at me and I smiled back at her. The whole exchange lasted three seconds, but there was a knowing when our eyes met.

Not every woman has whatever it is you must have to want and, yes, need to wear red lipstick. When I say red, I mean a true, stunning crimson. It was interesting to me that she was so young. Most girls her age are wearing ugly brown shades, a burgundy vampire color, or just clear gloss. True glamazons of any age wear red lipstick. Madonna, Sharon Stone, Catherine Zeta-Jones, and Nicole Kidman, to name a few. Red lips give color and life to the face, but it's not for the timid. And forget that balderdash about redheads not being able carry off red lips. Any woman who can handle the attention—and what Southern belle can't?—looks better in red.

Red is a sisterhood that binds certain women together. We love to find a new, perfect red lipstick. We know it makes us stand out and we are happy about that. We don't hold back with a demure peach or pink; we let our lips, and our smiles, shine out for all to see. I refuse to think of red lips as anything but sexy, powerful, and timeless.

Even so, at a certain age (meaning mine), one must be very careful in application or the effect is most unflattering, so I follow my "Rules for Ruby Lips" like the gospel. I know there are some closet glamazons out there, so please don't be afraid. Red rocks! Rules for Ruby Lips:

- Prep your lips first by using my favorite trick: Brush your lips with a soft toothbrush and Vaseline. You really want those lips to be plump and kissably smooth.
- Pat the area around your lip line dry. Too much foundation or moisturizer will contribute to "bleeding," a big fat no-no for red lips.
- Line your lips with a liner that matches the lipstick. Gently pat the liner dry.

- *This is one time you should use a lip brush because you want a perfect application. Avoid using too much lipstick or gloss, as this also contributes to bleeding.*
- *Perfect red lips should look neat, naturally moist, and be complemented by simple, understated eye makeup.*

—Adrienne Hemphill
Mississippi

A Silk Purse from a Pig's Ear

Although they'd never brag about themselves, each and every GRITS I know is a wonderful woman, and a real pleasure to know. Unfortunately, though these ladies are worth silk and pearls, sometimes the world hands them a tough old pig's ear. When this happens, GRITS move on and do the best with what the world gives them. GRITS try to live up to the Southern virtues, and they treat everyone they meet with kindness and respect, even if they don't receive the same back.

Now, I know that the most common version of the saying is "You can't make a silk purse from a sow's ear," but there's something about the word "sow" that I cannot abide. Mention certain words, and it's just like hearing nails scratching on a chalkboard. "Belly" makes me cringe, "sow" and "swine" just don't sit right, and I can't even mention s-n-o-t or f-a-r-t (I call that one a "fluffy").

The "pigs" in our lives take many forms. We have unemployment, bad marriages, sickness, leaky plumbing, and angry drivers, just like the rest of the world. The difference between GRITS and others is that GRITS learn to turn the other cheek—to put on a smile regardless of what the world throws at them.

We Southern girls are no strangers to adversity, and we've learned that staring down your problems is a lot easier with a girlfriend by your side. Here in the South, we've gotten through a civil war, dustbowls, poverty, and almost a decade without one of our sisters winning Miss America with the help of our friends. I think we can get through a layoff or a crying toddler without batting our perfectly curled eyelashes, as long as we keep our friendships in good repair.

Each chapter will include some tips for building and maintaining friendships, no matter what obstacles you face.

A Warm Smile for a Cold World

- When you greet a person who refuses to greet you in return, keep smiling and waving. She may be having a bad day, she may be distracted, or she may be a New Yorker. At least you can try to help her get over the bad day, and two out of three ain't bad.
- When your second mortgage is overdue, your husband is spending more time at the bar than at home, and you've backed your minivan into the lightpost, you may think that it's no time to make new friends. Sugar, I say it's the perfect time to meet new people, so always keep on a smile. No matter how busy you are, or how much stress is in your life, there's

nothing like meeting a new GRITS friend to ease the pain. Besides, when you keep that smile on your face, there's no telling what might happen. A case of whiplash in a car wreck just might lead to a date with that good-looking rescue worker.

- Believe it or not, some Southern ladies are embarrassed of their beautiful drawls. They're afraid that people will think that they're stupid, or that people will judge them, and they have some reason for those fears. I knew one woman who, when she opened her mouth at a cocktail party up North, was told she sounded like Gomer Pyle, and I know another who was told that she had great teeth . . . for a Southerner. Most of the time, though, you'll find that your voice brings a welcome note of softness to the conversation, and if people mention your drawl at all, it's to compliment you. So don't miss out on all the wonderful people you might meet because of a few fools who don't realize that we not only have indoor plumbing in the South, we have dentists who know how to use it. Open up your pretty little mouth and let out the sweet sound of the South.

- If, no matter how hard you try to reach out, you still get a frigid shoulder instead of a warm, Southern smile, move on. Since you're a GRITS, you'll always show a kind face, but you don't have to worry about impressing someone who isn't impressed with you. There are plenty of GRITS in the sea, honey, so don't go fishing for those bottom feeders.

CHAPTER 2

Mommie Dearest: Our First Friend

"You never realize how much your mother loves you until you explore the attic and find every letter you ever sent her, every finger painting, clay pot, bead necklace, Easter chicken, cardboard Santa Claus, paper lace Mother's Day card, and school report card since day one."—PAM BROWN

"How simple a thing it seems to me that to know ourselves as we are, we must know our mothers' names."—ALICE WALKER, *IN SEARCH OF OUR MOTHER'S GARDENS*, GEORGIA

A GRITS's first and most important friendship is with her mother. Mother is home, Mother is childhood and, to a lot of us, Mother is what we think of when we think of the South. To a lot of Southern women, Mother is their best friend. To others, she's that pain in the neck who just won't stop nagging, but everyone knows that the nagging is a mother's true calling. The friendship between a mother and her daughter is the basis for all the friendships a daughter will have in her life, and it's the most treasured, lasting friendship for a mother.

Add a Pearl, Drop a Pearl

Mother (and Daughter) of Pearl

A well-brought-up GRITS will always listen to her mother, and a well-brought-up mother will treasure her baby girl. Still, there comes a time when women want to stand on their own feet. As the younger generation grows up, it's hard to stop being mother and baby and start being friends. Set up a date with your daughter—get a manicure, have lunch, or take a long walk. Set a goal of offering her no advice for fifteen minutes (I know, I know, it's hard as rock candy);

concentrate instead on what she's saying. You may find it surprisingly hard to stick to your guns, but after a few "dates," you'll discover that you're speaking with a wonderful young woman who you're proud to call a friend.

Every mother treasures each gift that a daughter gives her, whether it's a masterpiece portrait made of macaroni and glue from an Instant GRITS or a diamond necklace from a GRITS who's all grown up. Don't wait for Christmas or her birthday to send her a little something to show you care. You don't have to break the bank. In fact, your mother may appreciate a handmade card that shows you took the time, and shows the love more than a box of chocolates or expensive flowers that took only money.

Sometimes, our mothers and our daughters are so close to us that we have trouble saying what's important. Try to sit down and write a letter to your mother or to your daughter, and tell her why she's important to you. It's often easier to give your love when you aren't sitting face-to-face, especially if that face is nagging you about when you're going to have her grandchildren. You don't have to be a wonderful writer; sincerity and honesty are more important than having a gift with words. A letter filled with love is sure to find its way into her most treasured possessions, and years from now, when she's feeling down, she'll unfold it and know that a special GRITS loves her.

Books for recording memories of your daughter from birth to adulthood are widely available. You and your daughter and, someday, your granddaughter, will treasure the memories that you record. And don't forget to include first locks of hair, first teeth, first theater tickets, and petals from her prom corsage.

The Magnolia Blossom Doesn't Fall Far from the Tree

Your mother is your first friend, and often the first woman you fight with. It's the most wonderful, and sometimes the most difficult, relationship between women. When a woman has a daughter, she realizes how important her mother was to her. Relationships between mothers and daughters aren't always easy, but they're worth the effort.

PEARL OF WISDOM

"My own mother learned well at her mother's knee and learned to be another splendid example of silk blended with steel." Rhonda Rich *in* What Southern Women Know, *Texas*

GRITS GLOSSARY

Mutha [məthə] n. *The only correct term a good Southern debutante uses for her mother. Given names are never applied to Mutha and, indeed, the true debutante may not acknowledge that Mutha has a given name. See also "Mama," but only if you've perfected that glorious Southern twang.*

I didn't sit for hours gossiping with my mother—she was too busy trying to bring up her children on her own to have time for that. I still remember the long hours she worked, inside and outside of the home. Our best connection was not through words but through sewing. Our common thread held us together, even if it took years for that thread to go through the eye of the needle. I was an adult woman before we really connected, and I think it was our mutual love of sewing, fabric, and creativity that finally stitched us together. Sewing was so important that I really wanted her sewing machine after she passed away, but she left it to my sister Rita. We argued over it, and I know that she has that sewing machine stashed away somewhere!

PEARL OF WISDOM

One way for Southern mothers and daughters to bond is to learn about their family history together. Make a "family tree," but instead of including just names and dates, include something meaningful for each person on each branch. First, fill in your family tree as fully as possible from your memory. Then, make a separate page for each person. On that page, include the person's name, birth and death dates, spouse, and children, and a photograph, if you have one. Then, write down any funny stories or facts that bring that person to life. Did he have any strange superstitions? Did she always make identical dresses for her daughters? Did he love pouring peanuts into his cola? Did she bake the best cornbread in five counties? This is a great opportunity for you and your daughter to speak to your relatives to find out more about your families and yourselves. When your pages are done, you can either pin them up on a free wall (or the free side of a barn, given the size of many Southern families), or you can place them in an album as a family keepsake.

Top Ten Reasons Your Mother Is Different from Any Other Friend

1. She's not afraid to tell you how your hips really look in those hot pants. The best way to keep your daughters from wearing trashy clothes is to show them how they look by wearing them yourself. My daughters would die if they saw me in a pair of hot pants!
2. You share a history with her the way you can with no other friend, and the two of you both know that Daddy is the most special man in the world.
3. When she says she's happy to look after the baby while you go out for the night, she means it.
4. Even if you've stopped looking for Mr. Right, she'll never stop looking for you.
5. She's the only person in the world who thinks you're prettier than Miss America.
6. There's a chance she'll share your grandmother's dumpling recipe with you someday.
7. She can always blackmail you with that childhood picture. You know the one I'm talking about.
8. She taught you the importance of taking care of yourself emotionally, spiritually, and financially. Whatever path you choose, she wants the best, and only the best, for you. She taught you to forge your own path, but to learn from her mistakes.
9. She has your eyes, your nose, your thighs, and a Thighmaster you can always borrow.
10. You'll always be her baby . . . loudly . . . in public.

My mother and I weren't close the way many Southern mothers and daughters are. Still, she's the woman I judge all other women by, including myself. I think of her often and with pride, and hope that if she saw me today she'd be proud. Our mothers shape us. They give us our eyes and our skin color (and, I'm afraid, our cellulite), and they also give us our character. Mothers carry forward our Southern traditions—they teach us respect, honor, hospitality, and generosity. My mother taught me to never chew gum in public and certainly to never smoke. She taught me to never use a toothpick—unless it's the frilly kind on an appetizer tray, of course. She taught me to never say an angry word in public, just as I taught my own daughters, and to certainly never air the family laundry.

WELL, I DECLARE

Louisiana GRITS Britney Spears and her mother Lynne are never apart for more than six weeks. Even this is too much for Mama to be separated from her international superstar daughter. She says: "She's my little girl and I miss her."

Most importantly, mothers teach us right from wrong—and make sure that those values are in our lives and hearts and not just on our tongues. When I was a girl, my mother forgot to pay for gas during a long car trip. We had to turn around, drive an hour, pay, and then get back on our way. She added two hours to our trip and burned a lot of gas, but she could look her children in the face with pride at the end of the day.

PEARL OF WISDOM

*"My mother is so Southern. She has all these sayings,
like 'Everyone's hair looks better with a few hot rollers in it,'
and 'The blonder you are, the better you look.' "*
—Reese Witherspoon, Nashville

WELL, I DECLARE

According to a Seventeen *magazine survey of 4,000 moms
and daughters, the majority of this generation of daughters feels
that their moms are their best friends. Forty-seven percent of daughters
and forty-three percent of moms said that they talk with each other about the
important topics in their lives. According to this survey, these numbers would
not have been as high forty years ago! Sixty percent of moms feel they have a
better relationship with their daughters than they did with their own mothers.*

Accent? What Accent?

*When I was in culinary school in Charleston, South Carolina, my
classmates were from all over the country, but few were from the
South. They thought I had a very heavy Southern drawl—that is,
until they heard my mother.*

*A group of us took turn turns hosting little gatherings at each
other's homes, and it was my turn. We were having a ball! We were
acting like adults with our crudités, cheese tray, wine and, of course,
imported beer. The whole group was laughing and telling stories.
Then one of them began ribbing me about how hard I am to reach.*

*They all began to chime in: "You're never home," "No cell phone,"
"You don't return messages." They were quick to point out as evidence
the blinking light on my answering machine. "Hey, do you ever check
those?" one of my friends said to me. "All right, all right," I said and
pressed the play button. There she was . . . Southern Steel Magnolia
squared, complete with a hint of sarcasm and guilt to boot!*

> *"Susan . . . this is your mother. . . . Linda! As far as your fa-
> ther . . . Lloyd Frank [who when my mother says it sounds like
> Lord Frank] and I know you are not deceased. We have been in
> touch with the troopers in Alabama, Georgia, and South Caro-
> lina, and so far no one has turned up in a ditch who matches
> your description. If you are still with us and you find you have
> time to contact us, we would appreciate knowing you were still
> breathing. . . . Bye, darling."*

*There was complete silence in the room. When I looked up in synch
with the telltale beep of the machine, I caught the very large eyes and
open mouths of my friends, who immediately broke into hysterical
laughter.*

—S. Greysen Emfinger
South Carolina

Thank Heaven for Little Girls

My mother always told me that no one would ever love me
like she did, but because we struggled with each other so
much, I never really was able to understand what she meant.
Then, when my daughters, the most wonderful girls and
now women that I've ever known, were born, I finally understood. Those perfect creatures could break my favorite vase,

could cry until the sun came up, could cut off their best friend's hair, but I would love them with a love so strong it seemed to fill up my whole body. And, of course, when they were between the ages of thirteen and eighteen, I could embarrass them to no end.

WELL, I DECLARE

Although Rosanne Cash, daughter of country music legend Johnny Cash, has had plenty of worldly accomplishments, she says that none has so defined her art or her life as having her daughters.

From Mama to Daughter

Every Southern mother wants her daughter to have fabulous friendships. It's our job as mothers to put our daughters on the right path.

- *Set an example by having warm and healthy friendships in your own life.*
- *Teach your children to resolve their conflicts without resorting to gossip or name-calling. Teach them to kill their enemies with kindness; it's the GRITS way.*
- *Keeping in touch can never start too early. When a young friend travels or moves away, or cousins go back to their own town, encourage your daughter to learn the almost-lost art of letter writing, or at least send an e-mail.*
- *As I'm sure you've told her a thousand times, your little girl won't meet anyone playing Xbox in a darkened room. Get her involved with a sport, a scout troop, or an after-school club.*

She may whine about losing her free time, but she'll thank you when she's swapping friendship bracelets and chigger bites at summer camp.

- *Encourage parties and sleepovers. You don't have to go all out and rent the movie theater for your daughter. In fact, she'll probably be happier dancing to CDs with her closest friends than running around some expensive store with dozens of children she barely knows.*

A Southern mother's love may be the strongest force in the world. We love our families, and we love our daughters even more. Our daughters are our lives and our loves. No husband, no sister, no friend will ever mean as much to us as our daughters: the light of our lives and of our worlds.

Lily of the Valley

Like a lot of Southern women, I love everything that grows, and I've learned to take the weeds and bugs that come with the beauty of the flowers and trees. Throughout my life, I've thought of my friends as flowers. Some are lilies, some daisies, some peonies. Some are strong like oak trees or gardenias. Some are beautiful but delicate, like those tea roses that always seem to have some critter crawling on their leaves.

My favorite flower is the lily of the valley, but I'd never thought of any friend this way until later in life. Finally one came into my life. She's been with me almost twenty-four years. I've thought of many growing things that remind me of her—some were nice, some were beautiful and, I admit, some were not very nice at all. After all of

these years, she's become my dearest friend, and I share the purest love
I know with her. She's my daughter, and I treasure her friendship. She
will always be my lily of the valley.
　—Mia Cather
　　Alabama

A Southern daughter might be sweeter than honey, but she can sting worse than a bee. There comes a moment in every mother's life when she realizes that her cute little baby has developed the personality of a Chicago cab driver on a rainy day. If she's been raised right, her tough months or years won't last long, but it's a trying time. It's hard to go from knowing everything to knowing nothing in your child's eyes. Even after adolescence, daughters still aren't always perfect. You have to wonder why she dates *that* boy, moves to *that* faraway city, wears *that* awful dress or, worst of all, still hasn't brought you any grandchildren. Children are the greatest blessing in the world, but sometimes they make even the best mother wonder if that child isn't the one and only reason for those gray hairs and pesky crow's feet.

WELL, I DECLARE

A Cambridge researcher studying mother-daughter arguments has found that frequent arguments may actually be good for the relationship. They may need to argue as part of the normal process of the daughter becoming an independent adult. So the next time your daughter screams at you for wearing your flowered sweater to her school, remember that she may be making your relationship better!

As our daughters grow up, we remain their mothers, but we can also be friends. I can tell you from my own experience that a daughter can be the most wonderful friend a mother can hope for, if she takes the time to get to know her as the fine adult she's become (and with a GRITS as a mother, she's bound to be pretty fine).

Top Four Tips from a Southern Mother to Her Daughter:

1. *If there is only one lesson I could give to my daughters, it would be this: Love and respect yourself.*
2. *While some advice, such as "ladies don't chew gum," might sound a bit old-fashioned, good manners never go out of style.*
3. *A mother's fashion sense never goes out of style. Find your own personal sense of style and stick with it, no matter what the trends are.*
4. *Always listen to your Mutha and always remember your way home.*

Top Five Tips from a Southern Daughter to Her Mother:

1. *Don't advise me on my clothes . . . unless I ask.*
2. *Don't complain about my man . . . unless I do it first.*
3. *Don't buy me any furniture . . . unless I casually mention I'd like to have it while we're out together.*
4. *Don't nag me about my choices, family duties, or being late.*

Be happy to see me, however I choose to be, and I'll be happy to see more of you.

5. *Let me be me.*

Looking for Trouble

Southern daughters—and sometimes their mothers—face troubles, but they are also good at making their share. We spend so much of our lives being good—taking care of men and other children, keeping ourselves lovely, treating others with the respect and kindness of a lady—that when we let loose and get a little bad, it feels extra good. Now, I'm not suggesting that GRITS misbehave, or ever act like anything other than ladies. We'd never do anything to make our mothers ashamed. I'm just saying that sometimes life means letting loose and acting just a little crazy.

The Royal Pig

This is one of my favorite stories about my mom.

Spring Fling was an annual fun-filled weekend all the students looked forward to at the University of North Alabama. There were chariot races, powder puff football games, and many other events in which members of the clubs on campus competed. One event was catching a greased pig. Because she was pretty athletic, quick, and small, my mother's girlfriends just knew she was the one who could catch that pig, and they signed her up.

Her date for the dance that night happened to be one of the best-looking guys on campus, and she was really looking forward to putting on her beautiful frilly dress and being seen with him. She was worried that he wouldn't be impressed by her chasing after a greased pig, much less catching it. Needless to say, she could not get out of the contest and let down her girlfriends. Being embarrassed already, she decided to go ahead and make it quick. She caught up with that little guy, jumped on him, and held on for dear life. Little did she know that a picture of her hanging on to that big ole greased pig landed on the front page of the Florence Times.

That night at the dance she was given a trophy for her slippery feat. The only saving grace happened to be that she was also chosen Homecoming Queen. Where else in the world can you catch a greased pig and still be homecoming queen on the same day?

—Callie Michael, daughter of Deborah Ford
Washington, D.C.

GRITS are ladylike and demure, and they always listen to their mothers. Beneath that gentle exterior, though, is a core of steel. We are, truly, steel magnolias. When a Southern girl knows that she's right, she isn't going to back down. Rosa Parks behaved like a lady, but when it came time to make a stand, she wouldn't give up her seat on the bus for anyone. With GRITS by our side, we know that we can make it through any kind of trouble.

*Even my own little girls got into their share of
trouble at school, but their hearts were always
in the right place.*

High Heels

My first real memory of school is preschool at the Birmingham Jewish
Community Day School. I wanted to look just like my mother, and
the only way I would happily go to school is if I could wear her
clothes. When I say that I wore her clothes, I mean I wore her dresses,
belts, jewelry: the whole shebang. Mom and I had the best mornings
getting ready for school together.

One day, Mom got a call from Ms. Linda, my teacher. I
wouldn't sing the songs, play at recess, or dance with the children. I
wouldn't even open my mouth to talk to Ms. Linda. She wondered if
something was wrong. Mom asked me and, sure enough, I was mad
as an old wet hen (as Mom would say). Ms. Linda had made me take
off my mother's high heels at recess! My mom finally convinced me to
forgive Ms. Linda.

Friendships are the most important relationships we have, not just
with our friends but with our family. One reason that my friendships
today are so strong is the example I had growing up with my mother.
Above anything else, she is my friend. No matter what crazy things
my sister and I could conjure up, Mom always made it clear that we
were free to live our dreams and follow our passions, even if that meant
wearing high heels to preschool. In my eyes, the most important gift a
mother can give is support for her daughter's dreams and wishes.

—Callie Michael, daughter of Deborah Ford
   Washington, D.C.

A Southern girl's first playmate is her mother. Teaching her to get out there and play—but still play nice—helps her to value and have fun with her girlfriends throughout her life.

A good Southern mother is part confessor, part fashion guru, part teacher, part cook, part drill sergeant, and part coach. Mothers help daughters grow by helping them to participate in everything from soccer to spelling bees. Southern mothers have always been at the sidelines to cheer their babies on, whether their girls are rough-and-tumble field hockey players or delicate ballerinas. Even when our daughters aren't at the top of their game, we still cheer them on. I had a very hard time telling my daughter Callie that she couldn't carry a tune, so my other daughter Chesley and I just sang all the louder to drown out the noise!

PEARL OF WISDOM

Although it's easy to just drag your daughter to your favorite childhood activity, your little tomboy may not be the tap-dancing whiz you were, and your quiet little lady may prefer sewing or painting to being a junior drama queen. Let her interests and personality be your guide. Push her to grow into the best person she can be, not into a mold of something she is not.

Playing together means hours together growing and sharing. It means holding her when she cries over being cut from the team or cheering until you're hoarse when she makes it. When I was a volleyball coach, I grew close to my girls because we spent hours working together and challenging each other. Mothers who stand on the sidelines while their daughters work and play can be both mothers and friends to their little girls.

Daddy's Little Girl

As close as Southern mothers and daughters are, no matter how much a mother teaches or how devoted she is to her children, there's always someone who comes first in a Southern daughter's heart . . . Daddy. Southern fathers dote on their little girls, and those little girls know it. For a mother who mends her little girl's cuts and bumps, who holds her hand on the way to school, who cuts the crusts off her bread just the way she likes, who combs the tangles out of her hair, it can be a little hard to watch that sweet little girl run off at the first sight of Daddy.

Your daddy is the first man to look into your eyes. He cares for, protects, and loves you unconditionally. Those of us blessed with growing up with a daddy had a foundation of love, acceptance, pride, and safety, the things that are the basis of any relationship. If you treat your daddy with love and respect, and he treats you with the same, you'll find that all friendships, whether with men or women, are easier. Daddies have a special responsibility. They shape a girl's expectations of all men. I often wonder if my own relationships would have been more successful if my daddy had lived longer than ten years of my life.

My own father became ill with cancer when I was about seven years old, and he was in and out of the hospital for the next three years. My sisters and I would take turns rubbing his feet, and he'd say, "If God's willing, we'll do so-and-so," (anything from cutting the grass to fishing). Daddy knew that he was dying, but he wanted to give us hope. He taught us that, even if we knew pain was ahead, we should always try to have hope.

GRITS GLOSSARY

Southpaw [sauth po] n. *1. a person who favors his left hand 2. the best kind of father in the world*

My Daddy

As early as I can remember, my father was everything to me. He may have been a civil rights leader to the rest of the world, but to me, he was just Daddy. He wrote in his journal that since the student demonstration had started in Montgomery, he had only a few hours of sleep a night. His rest was interrupted by the unfriendly telephone calls in the wee hours of the morning, the newspaper drop at three or four, and the cry of my brother for his bottle.

After a restless night, the daily 5:30 a.m. argument of his daughters over who would get to kiss Daddy first that morning made it clear to him that "the night had passed and gone, and that another day with its problems was at hand." The first problem was his daughters, who detested eating.

In between breaks of the Today Show, *he wrote that he would try to convince us to wait until Mother awakened later to make us breakfast. We didn't want Mother's breakfast, though, we wanted Daddy's. "Mother will only give us grits, bacon, milk, eggs, and toast. Or even worse, she might give us oatmeal, and who wants to eat that? What about you making us some sugar pop flakes? These are all right, 'cause Popeye says so on TV." He wrote that we pleaded, "Even if Mother gives us sugar pop flakes, she will not put in enough like you will . . . we think Daddy ought to serve breakfast instead of Mother—you know how to make sugar pop flakes taste so good. Please give us some now."*

He wrote that we were a "chip off the old block," so he most often would yield because he could not resist. "My daughters would forgive me and say, 'See you tomorrow, same time, same station.' "

—Donzaleigh Abernathy, daughter of Ralph David Abernathy, Alabama and Georgia

From the time he holds his baby girl to the time he walks her down the aisle (and later, of course), Daddy's little girl is his special child. We Southern mothers can only shake our heads and remember that he wouldn't be Daddy if he weren't special. Even if he's our ex, he'll always be a father to our little girl, and even if he isn't in our lives anymore, we have to thank him for that. Besides, you can always commiserate with your daughter when she discovers that Daddy has a new favorite . . . his little baby granddaughter.

He'll Always Be Daddy

Sometimes, marriages fail. Even if you don't get along with your ex-husband, he's your daughter's father, and you should do your best to get along with him.

- Even if his new wife has the personality of a Teamster, try to smile when you meet her. Your daughter is going to have to get along with the woman, and she'll take her cue on how to act from you.
- Even a man who thinks his recliner is a fashion statement and a burping contest is the highest form of entertainment is a wonderful daddy in his daughter's eyes.
- Remember why you fell in love with the man, bless his heart, and share those stories with your daughter. She'll love to hear about her daddy in the days before the bald spot and expanding waistline, and you'll feel better about him, too.

PEARL OF WISDOM

Every Daddy's little girl needs a pet name. If your husband needs a little creative inspiration, try sugar pie, honey bun, peanut, puddin', snickerdoodle, munchkin, pumpkin, squeezy, monkey, jelly bean, or bunny. Just make sure he doesn't say these when the boys are around, or he'll never live it down.

Tips for Daddies

- Listen to what your daughter thinks, feels, believes, and dreams. Don't just tell her she's pretty (even though she is!).
- Teach her to be strong by working to overcome obstacles; don't always try to remove them for her.
- Accept her for who she is.
- Play a sport—any sport—with her.
- Tell her you love her, and remember to show her as well.
- Treat her mother with love and respect. The best present Daddy can give is being kind to Mommy.

A Silk Purse from a Pig's Ear

Motherhood Madness and Daughter Disasters

- Not every Southern mother opens the door with a warm plate of cookies and an even warmer hug. For some Southern mothers, putting on a clean bathrobe is dressing to the nines, and serving a home-cooked meal means heating up the TV dinner in the oven. Not every Southern daughter brings home a successful husband and a beautiful granddaughter. For some Southern daughters, a weekend partying with her friends is the biggest commitment she can make. It's better to accept our mothers and our daughters for who they are than to expect them to be the model of Southern womanhood. Try to find the good things in your mother and in your daughter, and don't focus on the bad. Take the time to tell her one thing about her that you think is wonderful. After a while, you'll be seeing the wonderful things without even trying. None of us are models of perfection, but all of us have something worth loving.

- Schooling, jobs, and marriage often take mothers and daughters far apart. Living across the country doesn't mean that you can't be close to your family. Make a list of all of the important, or just interesting, things that happen in your life, and keep it by the phone so that you don't forget when you talk with each other. Though the phone bill might strain your mailman's back, call often. It might cost money, but the time spent hearing each other's voices is worth all the money on Wall Street. If you're a mother, take the time to learn e-mail and instant messaging; you'll be glad you did when you can send your daughter a message for any old reason, even if, after the tenth message of the day, your daughter prays for the good old days of snail mail.

- Fights between mothers and daughters can be far more painful, and damaging, than fights between other friends. After all, you can walk away from a friend, but mothers and daughters are stuck with each other. If you're a mother, try to remember how your own mother's words affected you, and resist the urge to say critical words. If you're a daughter, try to remember that you are the most important person in your mother's life, and what you say can hurt her more than the words of all of her friends combined. When in doubt, it's best to let criticisms that spring to your tongue never leave your mouth. Don't let words spoken in haste ruin a good relationship.

CHAPTER 3

We Are Family

"Is solace anywhere more comforting than that in the arms of a sister?"—ALICE WALKER, GEORGIA

"In every conceivable manner, the family is link to our past, bridge to our future."—ALEX HALEY

riends are important to a Southern girl, but family is sacred. In a time when people travel across the country, or even the world, for jobs, when new neighborhoods are sprouting up over the South like mushrooms after an autumn rain, when fast food and video games are replacing meal time, it's harder to maintain the kind of deep ties that we Southerners cherish. Making friends outside of our families is more important than it used to be, but that doesn't mean that we need to get rid of our family connections, even if, after hearing Uncle Wade's war stories for the hundredth time, we sometimes wish we could.

GRITS love their girlfriends, but taking time to make friends with their women kin is deeply important to them, even if sometimes they make us want to back-talk and roll our eyes like teenagers. Our relationships with our mothers, grandmothers, sisters, cousins, and aunts form the basis of our character. Our female relatives make us who we are, and they shape all our future friendships.

Add a Pearl, Drop a Pearl

Cherishing the Best Family Heirlooms: Your Family!

- *Keep out! No boys allowed! Big extended family gatherings are wonderful, but too often, the women end up spending all their time running from the kitchen to the table and tending to the needs of the men. Pack the boys off to the bowling alley or the big game, and have a gathering of just the ladies. You can have fun reminiscing or getting to know each other better, and you don't have to worry about the men complaining about the women sitting around gossiping like a bunch of hens.*

- *We Southerners have always taken pride in making things by hand. Our handmade items—quilts to warm chilly winter nights or preserves to bring a taste of summer even in January—are not only useful, but beautiful expressions of our art and ourselves. These talents have been handed down from mother to daughter for generations but, sadly, so many things these days are store-bought and disposable that some traditions are being left behind. If someone in an older generation still has these talents, take the time to learn from them. If, as is so often the case, the talents have died out in your own family, take a class or read up on sewing, knitting, pottery, candle making, canning—whatever strikes your fancy—and once you've learned the art, pass it on to your daughters, granddaughters, or nieces.*

- *In our rush to finish that report at work, drive our children to soccer practice, and put a hot meal on the table, we sometimes forget to take the time to tell our families how special they are. If you find yourself running around like a chicken with its head cut off, try to set aside at least ten minutes a week to do something for your family members. Don't be so ambitious that you don't meet your goal; a simple phone call or note is enough. You just might find that the time spent on family is really time spent on yourself as you take a break to smile and think of all those wonderful GRITS in your life and how much they mean to you.*

Birds of a Feather: Sisters

In my own family, Mother worked so hard that she often didn't have time for us, so my eldest sisters, Barbara and Virginia, became both mother and sister to me in a lot of ways. I don't think I would have made it at all in this world without the love, attention, and kindness my two older sisters provided for me. My sister Rita, on the other hand, was a lot closer to me in age, and we fought like cats and dogs. We even fought at my mother's funeral! We still don't see eye to eye, but of all my sisters, we probably have the closest bond. That's because with sisters, love and fighting go hand in hand.

A sister will always keep your secrets, even if it sometimes takes a little blackmail to keep that mouth shut. My first real boyfriend, Johnny, and I dated for four years. He wrote letters to me once, and sometimes even twice, a day during his first year of college. Even when we broke up, I refused to discard the letters I received from him. Like all Southern girls, I eventually had another boyfriend. When my new boyfriend and later husband found out I still had all of these letters, he demanded that I throw them away. He even wanted me to get rid of the beautiful cameo necklace Johnny had given me. Well, a man might ask a lot of things of a woman, but he's kidding himself if he thinks she's going to get rid of pretty words and prettier jewelry! My sweet sister, Virginia, took my big box of letters, placed them in her attic, and vowed to take care of them. To this day, she still has those letters.

I'm sure I know why she was so intent on keeping this secret for me: her fake ponytail. When Virginia met her husband, Julian, she was wearing the "ponytail." It didn't take her long to realize that he loved her long hair, and she found herself in a real dilemma. She was afraid he wouldn't like her if he knew her hair was short, and it would be even worse if he knew she was lying. She decided to wear that ponytail every time they were together until her hair grew out. Her hair did eventually grow and she was able to put away her fake ponytail and wear a real one. She made us all promise not to ever tell Julian her secret. We had so much fun bribing Virginia; we did it for years! Finally, after three children and fifteen years of marriage, my brother-in-law found out about his bride's secret. I think she just got tired of being blackmailed!

PEARL OF WISDOM

A sister is like a mirror. She might be a little chipped, or even cracked, but she reflects back what is good and what is bad in us.

Growing up, there was always someone we could go to when we needed advice on a crush, when we were fed up with Mother, or when we were worried that our breasts were too big, too small, or just plain funny looking. Sisters were always there when we needed them, or when we needed to "borrow" a blouse or a lipstick. A girl will usually have more history with her sister than with any other family member, even her parents. Sometimes we wished that our sisters weren't there, especially when they ratted us out to Mother or read our diary.

Guide to Sisters

Full: *We've got the same mommy and daddy, the same smile, the same problems, and the same hair-trigger temper, so do not make us mad.*

Half: *We've either got a different mommy or a different daddy, but we've got the same love for each other.*

Step: *Our mommies or daddies married each other, and once we learned to share the bathroom, we got a new friend in the bargain.*

Almost-Sisters: *Our parents were close and so were we. Whether we're cousins or just best friends, we have a bond that can't be broken.*

Soul: *Our mommies and daddies are different, but we've got the same grace, the same history, and the same spirit.*

Sisters of the South: *All GRITS are family, and like all families, sugah, you can never leave. And that's a promise, not a threat.*

WELL, I DECLARE

According to the U.S. Census, single-child families are the fastest-growing type of family in the United States. At this rate, it won't be too long 'til imaginary sisters are the only kind left!

We don't have to share the same parents to be sisters. Our cousins, neighborhood children, or even our friends from school can be the sisters in our hearts. What makes a sister a sister is that, even though she teases us and makes our lives miserable sometimes, she loves us in spite of our buck teeth and stupid jokes, and she'll stick by us through cheating boyfriends, bad perms, and tanning disasters. A sister will listen to us whine for hours, will teach us to pluck out those embarrassing eyebrow hairs, and will tell us all the good gossip when we're laid up with the flu. And that's why she's the most important tool in the GRITS bag of tricks—yes, even better than hot rollers.

WELL, I DECLARE

Big Brothers Big Sisters, an organization that provides mentoring to children, celebrated its 100th anniversary in 2004. Agencies exist nationwide, so if you want to make sure that a little girl has a Southern big sister to guide her along, look up the one in your community.

PEARL OF WISDOM

As much as we love our sisters, sometimes childhood wounds stand in the way of deep adult friendships with these special women. Getting that pain out of the way is the first step in becoming closer with your sister. Calling her up and telling her all the things that she's done wrong will do little to heal those rifts. Instead, try sitting down and writing all the things that she's done to hurt you. Then, dig deep and write down the things that you've done to her. You might find that even though she locked you in a closet for hours at a time, there were many other times that you "accidentally" let slip to Mother how late she came to bed the night before. When you're done, write down all the things that are wonderful about your sister. Then, tear, burn, or throw that paper down the garbage disposal; the last thing your sister wants to do is to stumble upon this writing. Getting your feelings out on paper will help you to stop dwelling on negative feelings. When you see your sister, think of all the wonderful things you wrote down about her, not about the bad.

In the end, it doesn't really matter whether you're sisters by birth, by marriage, or just by love. Any GRITS can become a sister. All it takes is love, caring, a warm shoulder, and endless patience. Sisters are fun, sisters are annoying, sisters know our secrets, good and bad. There's a reason that one of the most popular shirts my company makes reads: "Pearl of Wisdom . . . a sister is a girl's best friend." They're the joys in our hearts and the pains in our necks, but most of all, they're sisters, and that's a sweet word on any Southern girl's lips.

WELL, I DECLARE

During the War of 1812, President James Madison sent word to his wife to flee the capital; the enemy had broken through American lines and would soon enter Washington, D.C. Even though she could hear the battle in the distance, Dolley Madison took the time to write a letter to her sister: "And now dear sister, I must leave this house," she wrote, "when I shall again unite with you, or where I shall be tomorrow, I cannot tell!" That's Southern sisterly love!

Kissing Cousins

It isn't just our immediate family that we Southern girls treasure. When GRITS talk about family, we mean Great-Aunt Lettie, who's a bit teched, bless her heart. We mean those distant cousins who moved off to Chicago, poor dears. We mean everyone on the family tree, no matter how distant the branches, or how termite-ridden the wood. When you get down to it, we're all part of one big family, and Great-Grandma Eve would want us all to take the time to love each other.

GRITS GLOSSARY

Kissing cousin [kis-ən kuz-ən] n. *1. a family member that's not a sister or a brother, but who's close enough to kiss 2. the next best thing to a sister.*

Diamonds Are a Girl's Best Friend

When the girls in my family get together, we don't need fancy games and catered food . . . just a touch of Grandma's jewelry. Every year, we have a family gathering of all the women on my father's side of the family. This includes my mother, who usually spearheads the event. Our first year, we all met in Memphis, Tennessee, at my mother's home for a relaxing weekend of lying by the pool, cooking together, playing games, and drinking wine (those of age, of course!).

This particular weekend, there were three generations of Portis women. My father's mother, Dorothy Sue Portis, passed away about fourteen years ago, but her memory certainly lives on in our family and this weekend was no exception.

My aunts (my father's sisters and grandmother's daughters, Betty Ann Tanner and Leigh Ella Jones) brought Dorothy Sue's costume jewelry for us all to rummage through. We formed a circle around the jewelry and all took turns picking out our favorite pieces.

No arguments erupted, but there were a few funny comments when someone would pick a piece that another was wanting. After we picked all the jewelry, we all put our pieces on and wore them through dinner. We also started dinner with a prayer, saying what we were thankful for. By the time the prayer ended, we were all in tears (I'm sure the wine didn't help with that!). I think we all truly felt the spirit of my grandmother with us, and the joy of having such a close-knit family.

—Rebecca Portis
Tennessee

Woman's Best Friend

Sometimes we Southerners even include our nonhuman friends in our families. Dogs aren't just man's best friend; they're woman's best friend, too. I just don't know where I'd be without my little Alex and Poppsie. Dogs are full of love and devotion, traits a few more people could use these days. Besides, what woman wouldn't rather wake up with a soft, warm dog by her side than some stubble-faced man?

Ann B. Ross is the author of the well-loved "Miss Julia" books and a real live GRITS, and I'm pleased as punch that she was kind enough to share her delightful story.

The Tale of the Dog

I inherited Scooter when my son and his girlfriend broke up, and she returned everything he'd given her. John kept Scooter with him for a while, but in spite of announcing that the twelve-pound shih tzu with a sequined collar was his attack dog, his image as a fearless Atlanta police officer began to suffer.

Once, John was on his way home for a visit. He pulled off the interstate at a rest area to walk Scooter. Just as he nosed his Chevy Blazer into a parking spot next to another Blazer, his heart gave a leap. A gorgeous young blonde was leashing her dog for a walk. "A-ha," he thought, "I have a Blazer and a dog, and she has a Blazer and a dog. We just might have something to talk about." So he leashed Scooter and headed for the dog walk, all the while planning his opening remark. As John told it to me, his enthusiasm took a nosedive when he got a closer look. Not at the young woman, for she was as lovely as he'd first thought, but at her dog. "Mom," he said, "there she was with this huge German shepherd—seventy pounds if he was an ounce—and there I was with this fluffy little lap dog with a pink ribbon in his hair. I made a quick right turn at the first tree, told Scooter to hurry, and made tracks in a hurry."

So, by default, I became Scooter's owner, and thereby hangs a tale of sixteen companionable years.

I look back, now that he's gone, and recall his great heart: lion dogs, they're called in Tibet, where the shih tzu probably originated. He never cringed or ran from a larger dog; indeed, I often had to hold him back when we approached a lab or a shepherd or a collie on our walks. He never threatened these adversaries with angry growling or snapping. Instead, he would run up to a vicious-looking dog, stand his ground, and bark his head off, telling them, it seemed, to back off. And, interestingly, the bigger dogs usually did just that, wagging their tails, and giving him a sniff and a wide berth. And Scooter would prance away with his head and tail held high, confident in his authority and in his masterful handling of a dangerous situation.

But it wasn't only other dogs that he challenged, it was airplanes, too. The sound of the engine didn't seem to disturb him. In fact, he wouldn't even lift his head when he heard a plane—but seeing one was another matter. Each time he was outside when a plane came over on its way to the Asheville airport, Scooter went into a frenzy of barking until he'd chased it out of sight.

Never, though, did he bark at a child. As the grandchildren began to come along, we could find Scooter lying beside a crib or on a blanket on the floor watching over an infant. He allowed toddlers to roll on him and pull his hair, simply retiring to another room if the play got to be too much for him.

As for me, well, he and I grew old together. Our walks became shorter, our eyesight less sharp, and our steps slower. No longer was he interested in checking the bushes for the names and addresses of previous visitors. Squirrels and birds were allowed to go about their routines with hardly a glance, and other dogs to pass without notice.

A few months ago, during the time that a hurricane left us without power for five days, I saw that Scooter could no longer get to his feet. My little old man had made his last walk. In between visits to the vet, I wrapped him in my bathrobe that he loved, hand-fed him, and nursed him through the long days and longer nights. On our last visit to the vet, I held him in my arms as he went peacefully into his own long night.

I remember now how he kept me warm as he slept at the foot of my bed.

I remember now how, as a young dog, he followed me from room to room, wanting only to be with me.

I remember now how he rested on my feet as I worked for hours at the computer.

I remember how he would startle awake and look at me when I laughed aloud at something Miss Julia did.

I remember how, when I was away on a book tour, he kept watch beside the door I had left from.

I remember my little friend, who had the bravest and most loyal of hearts and, occasionally, I can still hear him call to me in the night.

—Ann B. Ross
North Carolina

A Silk Purse From a Pig's Ear

Fixing Family Feuds

Now, I know a GRITS like you would nevah, evah, call a woman in her family a "swine." Still, problems sometimes come up between female family members (and between males—but they'll have to figure it out on their own because this book is for my women friends!). It's best to try to nip those problems in the bud. Take some time for your female relatives, and have some fun doing it, and you'll find that you're closer than ever.

- *Pajama party! Invite the girls over for an old-fashioned pajama party. Play your favorite music, gossip about your significant others, drag out the Ouija board. Just being silly together can remind you why your sister, mother, or aunt is such a great lady, even if she's eighty!*

- *Love means never having to say you're sorry? Not on this planet, honey! I know it sounds obvious, but there's nothing like a good, heartfelt apology (and not talking back when she tells you how very wrong you've been) to make things all better.*

- *Get together with your family to "work it out": drag out your grandmother's chow-chow recipe and her dusty old Mason jars; pull out those boxes of family photos and a stack of new albums to put them in; or make an old-fashioned Sunday dinner for the whole clan. Spending a day treasuring your Southern family heritage can bring your family together.*

- *Give her a gift to let her know she's special. No, I don't mean going out and buying some little trinket, even a new string of pearls; save that for me, sugar! Tell her you want to baby-sit* her kids so that she and her husband can have time together; tell her you'll work on her résumé if she's getting into the job market; or cook her dinner and clean her house (but goodness, sweetie, don't tell her how messy it is) if she's been working late. The older mothers and grandmothers may appreciate a lesson in sending and receiving e-mail, but just be sure you keep that tongue in check when she tries to fit her best stationery into the disk drive.

CHAPTER 4

Leaning Over the Fence: Neighbors

"The good neighbor looks beyond the external accidents and discerns those inner qualities that make all men human, and, therefore, brothers."
—MARTIN LUTHER KING, JR., GEORGIA GRITS (GUY RAISED IN THE SOUTH)

"When women come together in one place to share their experiences, their dreams, and wisdom, a very special resonance, a powerful energy is created."
—MARION WOODMAN

There was a time in the South when family was everything in a Southern girl's life. Families gathered together to share made-from-scratch food in a kitchen that smelled of home, and they shared all the details of their days together. GRITS had friends outside of their families, but only family knew whether that was really Uncle Nathan's hair, that Cousin Dolly had a crush on the shoe salesman, or that every night you dreamed you had to take an algebra exam naked. Friends were special in a Southern girl's life, but blood ran far deeper.

These days, though family is still central to every Southern girl's heart, sisters, cousins, and aunts are often busy with their own lives and don't take the time they should for their families. In these times, we turn to those nearest to us—our neighbors and friends—for the support that family used to give.

Southern girlfriends are special, and they help us through every part of living, so there's no one I'd rather have on my block than a Southern girl. Good neighbors make your house truly a home. If you're a single woman, and you're bumping around your big, empty house by yourself, with a GRITS for a neighbor, you know that someone is always there to watch out for you. If you have a big family, you know that there is someone you can trust nearby when your children play outside. When you're making cupcakes for your daughter's class, and you run out of sugar at nine o'clock, you know your Southern neighbor will be happy to oblige. When you need to share, or you need a word of advice, you can always lean over the fence if there's a Southern girl next door.

Add a Pearl, Drop a Pearl

The GRITS Next Door

- *Working side by side can dissolve walls between people faster than most anything, and by working together, you and your neighbors can make your neighborhood a better place. Organize your neighbors to volunteer for a community service project together, such as adopting a stretch of highway. Or, if there's someone in your own neighborhood in need, such as an elderly widow whose family is distant, volunteer to help her out. A group of neighbors can repaint her house, or neighbors can take shifts to take her to doctor's appointments and other errands. Working together, neighbors can make their block the best in the city.*

- *I don't need to tell GRITS that part of neighborliness is keeping your home and yard in good order. The rusty pickup on the lawn and weeds growing in the gutter are sure signs that a GRITS is not at home. Go out and take a hard look at your house. Is it freshly painted? Is the lawn mown and edged, and free of old tires? If it is July, are all the Christmas ornaments down? Even the best home will have something in need of attention, even if it's only adding a splash of new color to your* old planting beds. Take the time to make sure that your house is one that the neighbors will be proud to have on the block.

- Children are your neighbors, too. Watch out for them when you drive down the street, and if they get a little rowdy sometimes, remember that kids will be kids. Mothers can volunteer to pool their resources on baby-sitting. Offer to take your neighbor's children when she goes out, and she can take your children when you're busy. Not only will you save on baby-sitting bills, you may just find a new friend. Children can warm the hearts of older neighbors whose own children have flown the coop. If you have young children, encourage them to be polite to your older neighbors, and suggest that they might even perform some chores—and cajole and bribe them if you must. They'll learn the art of neighborliness early, and your older neighbors will be glad to see a small, smiling face.

The New Kid on the Block

We Southerners are justly famous for our hospitality. When a new neighbor moves in, we're just itching to walk over there with a plate of warm peach cobbler and welcoming arms. No matter what our husbands might say, we aren't walking to our new neighbor's door to check out their furniture or find out their life story; we genuinely want to welcome people and make them feel comfortable.

WELL, I DECLARE

Our Southern hospitality is known so far and wide, we just can't keep people away! Between 1990 and 2000, the population of the South grew 17.3 percent. That's 14,790,890 new GRITS: Girls and Guys Relocated in the South!

Even though Southerners are always ready with a smile and a kind word, newcomers sometimes feel a little bit overwhelmed. Not everyone is used to waving and saying hello to everyone they pass in the street, knocking on a neighbor's door any old time, or offering a helping hand with everything from an oil change to a tree trimming. Some people are more used to squinting out of the peephole than opening their doors wide at the dog's first bark, bless their hearts. Believe it or not, some of our Northern neighbors have a hard time getting used to our sincere warmth. If you see a new neighbor, and she doesn't wave back, keep on trying; soon your warm GRITS smile will thaw even hearts frozen by the coldest Northern winters.

GRITS GLOSSARY

Newcomer [noo kəm ər] n. *1. In Atlanta, Charlotte, or Houston, someone who's lived in town twenty minutes; in the rest of the South, someone who's lived in a town twenty years. 2. A brand-new friend!*

A Cup of Cheer

Every Christmas, my mother-in-law's neighbor brings over a batch of her super-secret recipe for spiced tea. At first, I thought that the drink mix was a strange combination, but I grew to love it, and the tea has become a Christmas tradition in my mother-in-law's household. It's a wonderful way to warm up little hands on a cold winter day, or to warm up a new neighbor's heart. Although the neighbor keeps her personal recipe a closely guarded secret, with a little experimentation, I think that we managed a close approximation. I hope she's flattered that we took the trouble.

Bringing something homemade to your neighbors—even if it is something as easy as this recipe—lets them know that you care. If you want to meet your neighbors, but you can't think of any way to do it, no one will close the door to a woman with full hands and a warm smile.

—Elizabeth Butler-Witter
Florida

Stolen Spiced Tea Recipe

1½ cups instant tea
2 cups powdered orange breakfast drink
1 teaspoon cinnamon
½ teaspoon dry ground ginger
½ teaspoon ground cloves

Mix all ingredients together, and place in an attractive container. No, an old pasta sauce jar with half an old label just won't do in this case. Feel free to substitute sugar-free products if you're watching your weight or blood sugar. To serve, place a couple of teaspoons in a mug and add hot water. Stir and enjoy.

Southern Hospitality, Jersey Style

While planning our move from Up North to Down South, friends kept telling us about the wonderful Southern hospitality. The day we moved from Michigan into our house in Birmingham, Alabama, we experienced a taste of Southern Hospitality, Northern Style. Our neighbor came over to welcome us to the neighborhood carrying store-bought cookies on a Christmas paper plate. Did I mention it was June 30?

She had just moved in four days before us from New Jersey, and she was still unpacking and organizing. In fact, she told us we were lucky to get anything. No matter what she brought over, though, her gesture was appreciated. She has since become my best friend here, and together we are enjoying the South and all its hospitality.

—Ellen Knollenberg
Alabama

A Cup of Sugar and a Quart of Gossip

A good neighbor knows the history of everyone on her block. She can tell you why old Mr. McCrary drives his dog around the block four times every afternoon instead of walking him and where everyone's children went to college. She won't talk behind anyone's back, but she'll be happy to share the news, old and new. Everywhere a GRITS goes, she brings a bit of the old front porch with her. Her talk will bring a laugh even at the darkest moments, so when you've lost your job, your daughter's marrying a Bostonian, and you've broken your mother's vase, open up your door to a GRITS, and soon everything will feel fine.

PEARL OF WISDOM

We Southerners love our dogs, whether they're big old slobbery hound dogs or yippy little lap dogs. Although our dogs can be our best friends, however, they can be our neighbors' worst nightmares. Now, I hope that I don't have to tell you that you should show your neighbors consideration when it comes to your pets. Obey local leash and noise ordinances, and when your dog does his business on your neighbor's lawn, have the courtesy to clean up after him. GRITS make great neighbors, so it just makes sense that our best friends should, too!

Why GRITS Make the Best Neighbors

- Whether she lives in a double-wide or a white-columned mansion, her yard will be trimmed, her stairs will be swept, and her windows will be scrubbed.
- If a bulb on your Christmas lights burns out, run on over to her house. She's got strands on her bushes, her trees, and even the chimney, and she'll be happy to share the spirit with you.
- You'll never have to worry about your lipstick melting, your hair dryer burning out, or your last pair of stockings running; any GRITS worth her manicure will have a backup to loan you.
- She'll share her mother's squash casserole recipe, and if she knows how much you like it, she may even drop off a pan on your doorstep.
- Her ears are as wide open as the Mississippi River, but her lips are sealed.

The Banana Pudding Story

I was born in Beaumont, Texas, and my roots were deep in the East Texas Piney Woods. I have special memories of returning to San Augustine for visits with my grandfather, great-grandparents, cousins, aunts, and uncles. Families and neighbors were one and the same, and all were always ready to share the love and the spirit.

My special memory was a yearly spring celebration at Liberty Hill Baptist Church. Families, old friends, and members of the community would gather for Sunday morning worship, followed by dinner on the grounds. The gathering began early in the old wooden church. Paper fans from the local funeral home were passed out as we entered. A short sermon took place, and then it was time for a "singing" to the sounds of the old piano.

Just after the service, everyone gathered outside under the shade of the tall pine trees. Tables were heavy with homemade recipes from the whole congregation: fried chicken, chicken and dumplings, fruit cobblers, potato salad, purple hull peas, cream pies, and, best of all, my mom's banana pudding.

The Best Banana Pudding in the World, as made by Mom, Mrs. Lucille McEachern

½ stick butter
¾ cup sugar plus ⅓ teaspoon
2 eggs, separated
1 small can evaporated milk, plus enough whole milk
    to make 2 cups
1 teaspoon vanilla
2 tablespoons cornstarch
vanilla wafers, broken
3 bananas

Melt butter in a medium saucepan over low heat. Add ¾ cup sugar, egg yolks, milk, vanilla, and cornstarch. Whisk together and cook until it thickens, stirring often. Cool.

Beat egg whites with ⅓ teaspoon sugar until it forms soft peaks and set aside.

In a two-quart bowl, layer half the vanilla wafers, then half the bananas, then half the pudding mixture. Repeat and top with egg white mixture. Place in 350-degree oven until browned, about 5–10 minutes. Cool and refrigerate.

—Cathy Cooper
Texas

Clasped Hands

Neighbors, new or old, are there for us when family cannot be. When I was a girl, all my aunts and uncles, cousins, and grandparents lived nearby; today, we're lucky if even the nuclear family stays together. In this new world, neighbors have to step in where family used to: baby-sitting our children, helping out in the yard when we're ill or frail, watching the house, or picking up our mail when we travel.

PEARL OF WISDOM

"Better is a neighbor nearby than a brother far away."
—Proverbs 27:10

In a lot of ways, neighbors can be closer than family. An aunt or a cousin may just receive a notice when your child graduates from high school, but a neighbor will be there to give your child a hug and a big pat on the back. A neighbor can pick you up when you run out of gas and are stranded by the road. A neighbor will knock on your door and see that you're warm and safe after the big spring thunderstorm. GRITS are so full of love and caring that neighbors come to rely upon them, and even love them.

As much as I like modern times, sometimes I miss being in a place where I could walk down the street and be surrounded by a big extended family. With GRITS around, though, we can bring back a little taste of that old world. We can step up and offer aid to our neighbors, even when they're too proud to ask. We can show a friendly smile and give a loving word, even when our neighbors are giving us the cold shoulder. We can bring a little bit of family closeness to a place where neighbors are strangers. That's the GRITS way, and the South is a better place for it.

Sometimes, neighbors get into trouble a lot more serious than running out of gas or having the baby-sitter cancel, and those are the times when I'd rather have a GRITS for a neighbor than anyone else. When someone in your family passes on, a GRITS will be the first person knocking on your door with a shoulder to cry on and a casserole to feed your hungry children. When you lose your job, a GRITS will offer to keep your children while you interview, and will be happy to give you a makeover to help you out in the job market (though she'll also tell you that you don't need to get any prettier). GRITS are there when times are good, but they'll never run away when times get tough.

Some of the toughest times for Southern neighbors come

when our country goes to war. When men and women in uniform are called to duty, their husbands and wives are left behind with bills to pay, homes to maintain, and children to raise. During these times, you can count on Southern men and women to step up and offer a helping hand. I know one good military father who cut the grass, cleaned the gutters, and trimmed the hedges for his entire block when every other father on the street was called up during Operation Desert Storm. I hope that our brave soldiers know that their families are being watched over; that's the Southern, and the American, way.

A Silk Purse From a Pig's Ear

Would You Be, Could You Be, Won't You Be, My Neighbor (or Friend)?

Bringing closeness to your neighborhood is often difficult, especially in a new neighborhood where everyone is from somewhere else.

- *Getting to know your neighbors is sometimes just as easy as getting out to where they can see you. In these days of television and computers, families are often tempted to huddle together in their family rooms rather than get out into the fresh air. Honey, sitting in a dark room isn't doing any favors for your neighborliness, or your waistline. Take a long walk, play a game in your front yard, or just sit for a while on the front stoop. You'll be amazed at how quickly you're waving to the neighbors, and how quickly those waves turn into friendships.*

- Can't remember if the woman next door is named Karen or Kayla? If the woman down the street is a dentist or a veterinarian? Host a block party. Invite all the neighbors to a potluck in your yard or, better yet, if you can clear it with your city, on the street in front of your house. People are less afraid to visit if they know they can drift in and out when they want, and you don't have to host a high-pressure event. A couple of grills, a coolerful of drinks, and a stereo with upbeat music are all that you need. Your neighbors are likely to be as curious about the people they live near as you, so start printing up those flyers.

- People are often afraid that they'll be imposing on their neighbors by introducing themselves. I say, take the chance; the worst that could happen is that your neighbors refuse to open their doors. Goodness gracious, sugar, if we all sat around afraid to talk to one another, it would be a pretty boring world to live in! If you've lived in town awhile, and you still don't know anyone, or if those new neighbors seem standoffish, just march yourself across the street and say hello. If you feel you need an excuse to bother your neighbors, bake them some quick bread or cookies, and tell them that you wanted to share. If you just want to introduce yourself, though, it's perfectly fine to walk over empty-handed. Your neighbors are probably just as anxious to meet their GRITS neighbors as you are to meet them, so put a smile on your face, take a deep breath, and take the chance.

CHAPTER 5

The Care and Feeding of GRITS

"The solid rule of friendship: If you want a good friend, you need to be a good friend. Give away what you wish you were getting, and it will come back to you in spades."—DR. PHIL MCGRAW, TEXAS

"If all my friends were to jump off a bridge, I wouldn't jump with them, I'd be at the bottom to catch them. Everyone hears what you say. Friends listen to what you say. Best friends listen to what you don't say. We all take different paths in life, but no matter where we go, we take a little of each other everywhere."—TIM MCGRAW, HUSBAND OF A MISSISSIPPI GRITS AND FATHER OF THREE INSTANT GRITS

A deep GRITS friendship is the rock we cling to in troubled times. A GRITS friend can give you what you would have gotten from your sister years ago: advice, comfort, and a helping hand. And if you're a GRITS, you can give your friends the same. With a GRITS for a friend, you know that you always have someone to watch your back. A GRITS's door is always opened to her friends, even the ones with old tires and truck engines rusting in their yards. No matter who you are, she'll open the door with a big smile and wide-open arms.

PEARL OF WISDOM

"Friends are God's apologies for your families."
—*Wayne Dyer, Florida GRITS*

A friendship that is as close as family doesn't happen in just one day. Like anything worthwhile, it takes work. GRITS are willing to tend to their friendships, to give them the effort and time they take to grow. GRITS enjoy casual acquaintances, but it is the deep and lasting friendships that they most treasure. If you have a GRITS for a friend, you know you have someone who will take the time to get to

know you, and who will give your friendship everything it
needs to grow.

Helping a Friendship Put Down Roots
(Even in a Drought)

- Men give advice, women give an ear. When your friend wants
  to talk about her troubles, the best thing to do is listen, and
  then listen some more. Sometimes, all a woman wants or needs
  is a shoulder to cry on. Don't offer twenty ways to fix her
  problems; if she wanted someone who droned on and on about
  how she needed to fix herself, she would go to a man.

- The best way to grow a friendship is to give it time and
  opportunity. If you haven't spoken to your friend in a while,
  call her just to say hello. Find out what's happening in her life,
  and whether you can help with her pains or share in her joys.
  We're all busy, but nothing is as important as spending time
  with those who are important to you. Stay in touch, spend
  time together, but offer space for the friendship to grow on its
  own. In my experience, it takes about three years for a true
  friendship to mature and grow.

- Trust and honesty are essential to a close friendship. A real
  friend won't betray you and won't gossip about you and,
  above all else, will always tell the truth. If it's time for you to
  give up the heels and short skirts—if there ever really is such a
  time for a true GRITS—a friend will let you know. And she
  won't share that opinion with the entire neighborhood. She'll be
  gentle, but she'll be truthful. In my mind, even a white lie is a
  red flag.

- Take time to let your friends know that you care. I give my friends flowers for birthdays, anniversaries, and for just any old reason at all. A little note of appreciation, a small gift, or just a kind word of thanks will let the GRITS in your life know how important they are to you.

Share and Share Alike

GRITS know that there's a delicate line between sharing enough and sharing too much, and that the line moves as friendship deepens. If you've just made an acquaintance, and she's giving you the details of her colonoscopy, chances are, she's not a GRITS.

TALKING ALERT!

We Southern girls listen to our mothers, so we usually know when to keep our secrets close to our vests. Sometimes, though, even GRITS forget how much information is too much, so here are some guidelines on when to be careful with what we say.

Yellow Alert: Preachers and rabbis, therapists, taxi drivers, and dawgs. Share as much as you feel comfortable. These men and women are either bound to secrecy; have heard far worse stories than yours; don't speak a word of English; or are simply too busy scratching for fleas (not that I'd dream about gossiping about what's causing the good reverend's skin problems!). Whatever the case, your secret's safe with them.

Orange Alert: Bartenders and hairdressers. Keep in mind that a gossipy hairdresser is sharing not just with you, but with everyone who sits in that chair. And since a good hairdresser is worth her weight in styling gel, don't do anything to bust up that relationship. You don't want to be in dire need of emergency highlights when you realize that you can't face the man who knows you accidentally dropped your hairbrush in Aunt Edna's pancake batter before the big community breakfast.

Red Alert: *New friends. Sharing too much too soon can ruin a good friendship. Start slow—sharing that new needlepoint stitch is far different than sharing the family secrets. If you don't know her mother's maiden name, she doesn't need to know your marital problems.*

As the friendship becomes more intimate, information becomes more personal. If you're a real GRITS, you'll know that the best way to see if your new friend is ready for your secrets is to watch her. See what she reveals and when, and you'll have a better idea of when to take your friendship a step further. I don't need to tell a Southern girl that making someone else uncomfortable is a mark of bad breeding, and wouldn't make your mother proud. When your friends start to open up, when they start to share their own secrets in whispered tones, it's time for you to do the same.

PEARL OF WISDOM

One great way to strengthen both your friendships and your body is to share some time each day to walk or run with a friend. Not only will you keep your body healthy, dishing the dirt with a GRITS can make it fun. At first, you'll be sore in places you never knew you had muscles, and you won't talk about anything deeper than a shag carpet but, pretty soon, you and your new best friend will be sharing secrets and sashaying around in your new, fit bodies.

When you know you can trust your friend, and she knows that she can trust you, you'll feel more comfortable opening up to her. Trust goes hand in hand with honesty. Now, I'm not suggesting that you point out to your friend that she's grown as wide as a barn door, but if she asks if she could stand to lose a few pounds, a true friend might suggest going on a diet together. If she calls in the middle of the night, she needs to be able to count on you to pick up the phone, and not tell everyone from your hairdresser to the school principal what she called about. If you do what it takes to earn trust, you can always count on your GRITS friend to be by your side when you need her.

Real-Life Friends

Courteney Cox (an Alabama GRITS) and Jennifer Aniston were friends not only on a hit television show, but in real life. The two vacation together, live near each other in Malibu, and even spend the night at each other's homes. Although Aniston has said that Cox is a wonderful friend who can give advice in three seconds, both women are ladies enough to keep that advice private. They don't discuss their problems in public, only their affection for each other. When Jennifer Aniston won an award from ShoWest for Female Star of the Year, Courteney Cox took out a full-page ad in a Hollywood newspaper congratulating her.

PEARL OF WISDOM

You can shop around with all the phone companies that you like, but GRITS have the best phone plans: anytime, anywhere, any subject, unlimited minutes. If you have a GRITS for a girlfriend, you can always call.

Like the Back of My Hand

A GRITS knows everything about her close friend, from where she had her first kiss to the fact that her favorite diamond earrings are nothing but paste. She knows how proud you are that your son is graduating from medical school, and she starts bragging so that you won't have to. When your mother has passed away, she knows that you feel down on her birthday, and she plans to spend the day with you even before you ask her. She knows that an acquaintance has hurt you with a casual remark even before you know it yourself. GRITS know their friends' secrets, they know their moods, they know their joys. It seems sometimes that GRITS know their friends even better than they know themselves.

Quiz: How do you tell if a woman is a true GRITS friend?

Do you know what her nose looked like before she "fixed her deviated septum"?

Do you know the name of her first boyfriend, even though she'd like to forget it?

Do you know what she looks like before she "puts on her face"?

Have you helped her move into a new home?

Have you talked with her about that man she's never quite forgotten, though heaven knows she loves her husband?

Do you find yourself whispering behind your hand and giggling with her, even though you're both in your sixties?

Do you feel comfortable letting her see the stretch marks, the cellulite, and the parts gravity has had its way with?

If she doesn't have stretch marks, cellulite, or parts gravity has had its way with, are you still on speaking terms?

When you ask what you look like in your new little black dress, can you count on her to tell you the truth?

Do you know what her real dream in life always was?

Do you know which child she loves most, though she'd never admit to playing favorites?

Do you know what worries keep her up at night?

Do you know her faults, and love her for them?

If you answered yes to more than three, count yourself a true GRITS friend, honey!

GRITS *share everything with their friends,*
even "last meals."

Sally Jean's Last Meal

The doorbell rang just as I was cutting up the last of the okra. Surely it must be Sally Jean; she was supposed to have been here an hour ago. How did I forget to leave the door unlocked, anyway? My hands were sticky from the okra, so I used a hand towel to open it. We greeted each other, and she surprised me with a gallon of her famous sweet tea. Sally and I had been friends since we were twelve years old, and today we were cooking up all of her favorites for her last meal.

Every burner was fired up on the stove, and we took turns tending to cornmeal-battered summer squash, fried okra, green beans, corn scraped off the cob with real butter and cream, and new red potatoes. The timer buzzed on the oven, and we pulled out buttermilk cornbread baked to perfection. Sally Jean turned off the Crock-Pot and opened it to the smell of pot roast so tender it was falling to pieces. We sliced home-grown tomatoes, garden-fresh cucumbers, and sweet Vidalia onions.

I dug out my best tablecloth and spread it across the dining room table, and we set out my best stoneware in true Southern style. Sally Jean poured out the sweet tea and squeezed in juicy lemon wedges. I pulled a work of art in a Pyrex dish from my fridge: layers of vanilla wafers and bananas drenched in the sweetest pudding I've ever made, topped with browned meringue.

Sally Jean was touched. Banana pudding had been her favorite dessert for twenty years. She sighed; both of us knew this was her last meal.

Sally Jean said grace in a voice barely above a whisper, then the eating and fun began. We ate and talked and promised to be best friends forever.

We toasted this last meal together with the clinking of our sweet tea glasses. It was the end for Sally Jean; tomorrow, she'd begin her diet.

—Sharon Bohannon
Georgia

PEARL OF WISDOM

"I now understand, at long last, that in a great relationship you can still maintain all the things that make you happy. I think a lot of my misunderstanding of relationships was in thinking I had to evaporate to be someone's girlfriend." Julia Roberts, Georgia

Part of knowing your friends so well is that you know that they aren't perfect: she may brag about her own children a little too often for comfort, pass off store-bought desserts as her own, and try to fit into pants she shouldn't even have worn five years and five pounds ago. GRITS accept their friends for who they are, and they aren't willing to lose them over dumb mistakes. A Southern woman would never stop talking to a friend over a slight. If she hears that a friend has been talking behind her back, a Southern girl might be hurt or angry at first, but if she's well brought up, she'll ask herself whether she gave her girlfriend cause to talk about her.

We Southerners don't sit around feeling sorry for ourselves—if we did, we'd never have come through war, racial tension, and the occasional losing football season to be the wonderful region that we are—we pick ourselves up, dust ourselves off, and start over fresh. I love GRITS, but I know that I, and they, aren't perfect. A Southern girl knows that real friends are few and far between, and she's willing to forgive a friend, just as she'd like to be forgiven herself.

PEARL OF WISDOM

"Friendships are like trees . . . they gotta bend both ways." Philip Kemp, Alabama

WELL, I DECLARE

Forgiving your friends may not just be good for your relationships, it may also be good for your health. Researchers have found that subjects who were more likely to forgive had, on average, better health, including lower blood pressure and better sleep, than those subjects who did not.

Love in Gray

Getting older meant that I started to understand the color gray, thanks to my cousin Ruth. I adored Ruth. She was eight years older, and since birth I had thought that she was one of the most beautiful people in the world. When we were little, my friends and I would play "pretend," and instead of fighting over who got to be Cinderella or Snow White, we would fight about who got to be my cousin. I was so proud to actually be related to this Tennessee legend.

When I was a freshman in high school, my mother said she had some news and told me that Ruth had gotten married over the weekend. I was crushed. I had always expected to be a bridesmaid in her huge wedding. I was so mad that she had done something so stupid. Several weeks later, I found out that Ruth, a senior in college, had gotten pregnant! I was disgusted with her. Things like that didn't happen to people like us! Our great-grandfather was our small town's mayor for twenty-five years. We owned the town's oldest manufacturing firm. We did things the right way.

Word traveled around our small town like wildfire, and I was so embarrassed. The next month, at a family wedding, I didn't even want to look at her. A few months later, Ruth got divorced, and I responded by rolling my eyes. I had very little to do with her pregnancy. I went to a shower and helped pick out a gift when the baby was born, but I really just wanted to avoid the situation . . . until I met her baby boy. From the start, he has been one of the most amazing creatures I have ever known. During the rest of high school, I became very close to Ruth and her perfect little son. Eventually, I understood the complexity of my cousin's situation.

One day, I told Ruth how much the whole situation had affected me. She understood, and we reasoned that this was my first mature experience with gray. My whole life had been a series of black and white, and right and wrong. Smoking, drinking, using drugs, lying, cursing, and having sex before marriage were wrong. I had never seen, known, or allowed for gray.

I told Ruth this, and she said, "Ya know, Laura, you grow up pointing fingers and casting judgments, and then at some point, you hope that you'll realize that you would rather use your hand to help someone than to point at them and tell them what they're doing wrong." She was right, and I have never forgotten those words. That desire to help rather than criticize has become part of who I am. The experience is a constant reminder that life is very seldom black and white, and is almost always gray.

—Laura Lefler
  Tennessee

Would You Like Some Whine With Your Dinner?

True friendship doesn't fade away in hard times; it just grows stronger. You can count on GRITS to be there when times are tough, and when the tough times have passed, they know their friends better and appreciate them more. Southern men might think that we just like to hear ourselves talk, but Southern women know that whining about problems helps us get through them. We aren't just shooting the breeze. We're strengthening ourselves, working our way through problems, and becoming better friends. Research shows that the tendency in women to talk through problems and to have deeply emotional conversations is directly responsible for their longer lifespans. So next time he makes fun of you, make fun of him for keeping everything bottled up inside. After all, which is the smarter, healthier approach?

PEARL OF WISDOM

"The best way to mend a broken heart is time and girlfriends."
—Gwyneth Paltrow

The Longest Six Weeks of My Life

When my son, David, called to ask me whether Sharon, who was working as his family's baby-sitter, could stay with me for six weeks while living arrangements for her and his family were settled, my only question was: "Can she cook?" She could, and Sharon moved into an apartment in my home while David's house was finished. After David's new home was complete, the plan was for Sharon to move out and into a condo that his family owned.

Sharon was a joy to have around, and at the end of those six weeks, my husband, Rush, suggested that she stay on with us rather than move into the condo. I had always said that if my ship came in, I'd have someone drive me everywhere, and Sharon was more than willing.

Sharon always kept me in stitches. She used to walk in the door and say, "Come on, let's pick up Helen." The two of us would pick up my friend Helen, and the three of us would do all sorts of things. Helen and I loved to shop, but Sharon could beat us both. The three of us would take trips to Hilton Head, and we always loved each other's company.

Sharon had a strong but friendly personality, and she ended up in charge of most things she touched. Before working for my son, Sharon had been at a bank for thirty years, and she had been a highly valued employee. She ended up going back to the bank to work, but even though she no longer worked for the family, she still stayed with us as a friend.

When my husband was ill, he asked Sharon if she would stay with me after his death, and she agreed. Sharon had become almost a member of the family. The two of us ate our meals together. When she returned from work in the evenings, we'd talk like the dear friends we had become. I struggled with the death of my beloved husband, but her friendship eased that pain.

Unfortunately, Sharon was diagnosed with cancer when she was still a young woman. During her illness, Sharon said that she should be the one taking care of me, but I cared for her just as I would any other family member. Cancer took her within two months of her diagnosis, and I still grieve for her. It hurt watching her slip away, but I was glad that she didn't have to suffer any more than she did.

Sometimes, friendship comes in unexpected ways, but it's no less a blessing. Those first six weeks stretched out to be eleven years. I still remember Sharon with love, and I think that I always will.

—Whitney Nicholson
Kentucky

PEARL OF WISDOM

To help a friend going through a time-of-life change or a crisis, such as a divorce or a child going away to school, take out a pile of old photographs of family and friends. Sit down with your friend, and help her make an album or wall of photographs. Looking over those pictures together will help her to relive memories of the good times, and help her get through the bad.

Though they'd never tell you themselves, the GRITS I know always look beautiful, poised, and friendly. But GRITS know that this is just the face we show the world. Every woman, GRITS included, goes through times of trouble, and in those times, her girlfriends are at her side.

PEARL OF WISDOM

When loneliness and grief are freshest, words should be the fewest.
Many times, the best help that you can give a friend is just to be there.

Every successful woman has a friend behind her, because even successful people stumble. We all have men who leave us, cars that break down, bills that go unpaid, dogs that vomit on the carpet right before our mother-in-law arrives. We all have those moments when it seems like nothing else can go wrong, and then it does. We see that famous starlet, smile glued to her perfectly formed face, and we think that she's always been perfect; that's just because we couldn't see her the day before when she backed her new car into the parking barrier and her face broke out in pimples. Your friends help you through heartache, money troubles, and troubled times. They give you the greatest gift GRITS can give to a friend: open ears and open arms. They tell you that things won't always be bad, and when it's a true friend, you sometimes believe them.

PEARL OF WISDOM

"It's your friends you can call up at four a.m. that matter."
—*Marlene Dietrich*

Though friendship grows in times of trouble, the mark of a true friend may not be that she helps you when you're down; it may be that she helps you when you're up. GRITS know that when one girlfriend rises up, we all rise up. If you're a true friend, you won't mind if your girlfriend wins the lottery, loses twenty pounds, and starts dating that fine-looking plastic surgeon. Oh, all right, you'll mind a little—you are human—but you'll also be truly happy for her. A true friend won't mind when you get the new BMW, even when she's still driving a beat-up old Datsun. After all, she knows that she'll be in your passenger seat, helping you to paint the town red.

PEARL OF WISDOM

"True friendship is a plant of slow growth, and must undergo and withstand the shocks of adversity before it is entitled to that appellation."
—George Washington, Virginia Guy Raised in the South (GRITS)

Sewing a Friendship Quilt

GRITS are by their friends' sides when the money is rolling in and the men are calling; they're at their friends' sides when there are no jobs and the bill collector is on the line; and they're at their friends' sides when nothing's up except the taxes. GRITS let their friends know that they matter in times of crisis, in times of joy, and just any old time. GRITS take time to let their friends know that they are special. Just taking the time to let a woman know that she matters to you can help deepen any friendship. It's your time that matters, not whether you give something perfect. A real friend will appreciate a simple bottle of her favorite nail polish and the offer of an hour to give her a manicure, as much as the fanciest handcrafted cake (especially if I'm the one doing the cooking, sugar). There's nothing like being loved to inspire love in return.

Friendship quilts are an old Southern tradition. A group of women friends pieces together a quilt out of old fabrics, and each seamstress signs her square. The recipient of the quilt has a token of friendship, and she realizes how truly special she is to those around her. Making a friendship quilt is a beautiful tradition, whether it's many women or just one doing the quilting. Collect pieces of old fabric that are meaningful to you—that T-shirt from the first race you ran together, a piece of your prom dress when you and your best friend danced the night away, a piece of that brightly colored blouse you wore to every game to cheer on the home team—and sew them together into a quilt of friendship and memories. Anyone receiving such a beautiful gift will realize how much she means to you.

GRITS GLOSSARY

Friendship ball [frend-ship bol] **n**. *An empty, decorative container that is filled with a small gift, then given to a friend. The ball is saved and passed back and forth through the years. Though based on a traditional ball, any empty container can be used, as long as it is given, and regiven, in friendship. Not to be confused with a friendship bawl, which is the best, most heart-touching kind of crying there is.*

Digging Deeper

- *A genuine friendship is reciprocal. No matter what she's going through in her own life, a GRITS will take the time to listen to her friends. If your daughter is getting married, and all your friend can talk about is her botox injections, it may be time to move on to someone who cares.*

- *When a friend hurts you, take the time to look closely at yourself. While a well-brought-up woman does not talk behind others' backs, that kind of talk happens for a reason. Look closely at yourself, no matter how painful it might be, and see if you're partially at fault. It's easier to forgive others once we realize that we need to be forgiven ourselves.*

- *Like all women, GRITS feel neglected and unappreciated sometimes. I've always felt that people get back what they give. Take some time to tell your friends what they mean to you, to give them a little gift of appreciation, or to say something nice about them. When you send out love, you'll soon see it flowing back toward you.*

- *If you find that you meet people quickly, but that lasting friendship isn't developing, you may just need to bring up every person's favorite subject: herself. Dale Carnegie said: "You can make more friends in two months by becoming interested in other people than you can in two years by trying to make them interested in you." If you want to grow closer to a friend, spend time asking her about herself. Pretty soon, she'll think that you're the most fascinating person she knows.*

SECTION 2

Living Your
Friendship

GRITS and their friends appreciate all the ages of a woman's life: "dippage, wineage, beerage, nappage, herbage, snackage, boobage, spaceage, slippage, and much much moreage."—JAN SIMMONS WITH MICHIE WENZLER, *THE CALL OF THE WILD*

CHAPTER 6

Girl Crazy! Playing With Your Girlfriends

Caro: "There's not a . . . breeze in the entire state of Louisiana."
Vivi: "Girls, we can not sit here and just puddle. Teensy, get your keys, we'll make our own breeze."
—*DIVINE SECRETS OF THE YA-YA SISTERHOOD*

"Grief can take care of itself, but to get the full value of joy you must have someone to divide it with."
—MARK TWAIN, MISSOURI GRITS

outhern friendship is about standing together with your friends, whether they've just been promoted to senior vice president or they've just taken out a second mortgage on the trailer. Sometimes, though, friendship isn't just about support, listening, and sharing; it's about laughing, playing, and just having a grand old time. GRITS treasure laughter, and I think the giggle of a Southern girl could just about charm the bark off a pine tree. Sharing joys, pains, and secrets with a Southern girlfriend is wonderful, but there's nothing I like to share with a friend more than a laugh.

GRITS and Giggles

- Remember, boys are made of snakes, snails, and puppy-dog tails. Organize or join an all-female group to share your interests, your hobbies, or just to have a plain old good time. If you don't have a group of close friends you can call, look for or post a notice at a local store, community center, or on the Internet. With a little work, you'll find a group of knitting grannies, Methodist kickboxers, single manicurists, or just a group of Southern ladies who want to have a good time.

- Getting the men in our lives to don formal attire, or even take off those muddy old boots, can be as hard as pulling a tooth from a grizzly bear, but girls raised in the South will pull out their finest for any old reason. Host a "glamour GRITS" night. Light the candles, polish your finest tableware (or borrow it from a friend), and pop open the champagne. You and your friends can enjoy the night, and your men won't spend the evening pouting in the corner. If you don't want to ruin that manicure before the big night, just grab some takeout to bring along; it isn't about the gourmet food, it's about feeling like a belle with the finest ladies you know.

- Even if you've spent the day battling traffic, a pile of work at the office, and children who treat your living room as their own personal Daytona 500, you can still find humor if you turn to our wonderful Southern artists. Grab a girlfriend and rent Divine Secrets of the Ya-Ya Sisterhood, Fried Green Tomatoes, or a DVD of a Southern comedian, such as Jeff Foxworthy or Brett Butler. If you have the time, get a women's reading group interested in the works of Southern writers such as Eudora Welty or Fannie Flagg. Even the more serious works of Southern literature have humor in their heart. After all, Pat Conroy, one of our best-known novelists, said: "My mother, Southern to the bone, once told me, 'All Southern literature can be summed up in these words: On the night the hogs ate Willie, Mama died when she heard what Daddy did to Sister.'"

- When GRITS are in the hospital, whether it's for a serious ailment or a little nip and tuck, nothing helps them to heal and get back to life as much as laughter. While flowers are the most common gift to hospital patients, and the thought is often *appreciated, a bouquet of daisies doesn't pass the long hours stuck in bed. Your favorite humorous novel, or just a good book of jokes, will help keep your friend in stitches or, better yet, get them removed sooner.*

Peas in a Pod

Whether we're little spoonfuls of Instant GRITS or big heaping bowlfuls of the real stuff, Southern girls know that anything is more fun with your girlfriends by your side. It doesn't really matter what GRITS do, as long as they do it together. We can bring meals to shut-ins. We can host a prayer group. We can get competitive out on the tennis court. We can shop 'til we drop. Whatever we choose to do, our time will pass a lot more quickly, and be all the richer, because we spend it with our girlfriends. We're like little peas in a pod, and we just don't have as much fun rolling along on our own.

Marbles and Misdeeds

Growing up on a farm in rural North Carolina, we had a lot of fun. I grew up on an historic farm in North Carolina, and though our life then might seem hard today, I wouldn't trade that childhood for any other. My parents were deeply loving and wanted us to have fun. During the summer months, when friends came to visit, we played marbles. We drew a large circle in the dirt, then each player placed their pile of marbles just inside it. Then we'd choose our best "shooter marble" to try to knock our opponents' marbles out of the circle. The objective was to hit out as many marbles with one shot as possible, kind of like pool. Sometimes we had a heavy steel marble called an "aggie" to shoot with, and then the game was faster and more interesting.

A little branch of water flowed through our property to the creek below our house. When our friends came over, we often dammed up the water to make a knee-deep wading pool. Then we hitched up our dresses (we had no pants, shorts, or bathing suits), and plunged into the cool water.

Our friends also joined us in romping through the woods, especially in fall and winter. We gathered beautiful leaves to make scrapbooks, checked the rabbit boxes to see if one had been caught for making rabbit stew, and searched for the perfect cedar tree for Christmas.

One Halloween, as my brother finished milking the cow and started down the path to the house at dusk, I donned a white sheet and hid in the bushes. When I jumped out, it scared him so badly that he spilled the milk. That was so much fun that I don't remember being punished for my misdeed—though surely I must have been. When a prank is really fun, it's worth even the inevitable punishment.

—Joyce Keever
North Carolina

PEARL OF WISDOM

If life is a bowl of grits, your girlfriends are the heaping pat of butter on the top that makes it taste so good.

Friendships, and what we think of as fun, change through our life. When we're Instant GRITS, there may be no greater fun than staying up past nine, weaving friendship bracelets, and dancing to our favorite songs. When you get to be on the fun side of fifty, staying up past nine is once again a big night with friends, and though we prefer gold bracelets to woven ones, there's still nothing quite like dancing 'til the men go home.

Roaming the hills and creeks of our childhood may become "hiking" once we get older, but it's that same love of getting back to nature and breathing the Southern air that sends us out into the woods—or walking around the local golf course. Instead of bopping to record players in our rooms, we may be slow-dancing at the country club or honky tonk, but it's the same rhythm in our souls. Well-seasoned GRITS may have more fun at the mall than at the jungle gym, but that same sense of play, and love of our girlfriends, stays with us all our lives.

TGIF Time: Thank God It's Friends Time!

When we're children, laughter seems to flow from us naturally, but when we're older, sometimes it's a bit harder to just let down our hair and giggle. When dignity gets the best of us, our girlfriends give us the courage to act silly and just have fun. Walking down the street playing a kazoo would make any well-bred woman blush with embarrassment, but marching with thirty of her best friends as the local kazoo band in the Fourth of July parade is fun for women from eight to eighty, and even beyond. Having a GRITS by your side gives you the support you need to laugh and love life, whether you're a toddler taking your first steps or toddling along on a walker.

Lucy & Ethel

As a true Southern belle, I have to admit I've never been one to forge or cultivate too many friendships with girlfriends. I've been quite content to nurture the friendships I have with my man friends instead. I find them less likely to engage in a catfight when push comes to shove. But that wasn't the case with Rhonda; that friendship was instantaneous, explosive, and intense!

Rhonda and I shared a love for the important things in life: shoes, jewelry, clothing, hours on the phone, fine dining, intellectual pranks, covert revenge, and the ultimate high—shopping! We knew where all the most highly worshipped meccas (malls, for the uninformed) were located within a day's driving distance, and it was no big deal for us to rise early and go on a whirlwind tri-state shopping spree and still be home in time for dinner—out with friends, of course!

We shared secrets, clothes, and the sheer love of making a credit card reach the maximum point of swipes without melting in the shortest amount of time. Practically from the moment we met at work, Rhonda and I were inseparable. She was a redhead, and I a blonde; we were the Lucy and Ethel of our time, only with more grace, better style, and a lot more moxie!

Without prior knowledge, we actually lived in the same apartment complex when we met, so proximity led to a lot of fun, a lot of laughs, and a lot of shared moments alone and with friends. Sadly, due to a series of misfires and circumstances—job changes, buying houses, and distance (among other things)—situations allowed that beautiful bond to slowly fade out of my life. I have to say, those were some of the best years of my life and I miss her still! Rhonda, if you're reading this, I will always love you.

—Susan Reno-Gilliland,
Georgia

With a GRITS girlfriend by your side, you can always have fun, whatever happens in life. Every woman faces hard times. Whether her last child flees the nest, her husband decides fishing is more important than marriage counseling, or she's had so many chin lifts that her ears meet atop her head, GRITS know that laughing at life with a girlfriend by your side is sometimes the only way to face your problems, or at least avoid them until tomorrow morning. Whether fortune is shining your way, or she's giving you the cold shoulder, Southern girls try to keep a smile on their faces. At the end of a long and brutal workweek, a Southern girl can always say: "TGIF Time: Thank God It's Friends Time!" and she'll know that everything is going to be all right.

Serious Fun

Getting out the stress while shopping, gossiping, or just vegging out in front of the television is important to friendship, but fun can be a lot more serious. Take time to deepen and grow your friendships while still laughing and having fun together.

- *Arrange a birthday or anniversary party in honor of your friend's elderly parents. Talk to your friend about their interests, and raid her home for pictures and keepsakes. Make or buy their favorite foods, and set the table in their favorite colors. Copy some of your friend's pictures of her parents, and place one or two at each place setting. Set a "memory table" of special photographs and keepsakes from their years together. Invite your friend's family and her parents' close friends, and ask guests to say a few words in honor of the parents. You will* learn more about your friend, and everyone will go home with another happy memory from lives well lived.

- Share the responsibilities and costs of bringing up your children together. After a week on the job, running errands, and balancing the family finances, every woman needs a couple of hours to herself or with the man in her life, but few of us trust the fourteen-year-old down the street to watch our children. Alternate taking each other's children for a couple of hours on the weekend. Trade used children's clothes, at least until the kids start to turn up their noses at hand-me-downs. When you shop at a warehouse store, and can't see yourself buying ten pounds of chicken or twenty cans of pineapple, bring along your friend, and split your purchases down the middle. Running a household is never cheap or simple, but with a friend by your side, it can be a whole lot easier, and a whole lot more fun.

- Whatever your religion, find a friend who shares your faith. Plan to meet once a week to discuss your religious journey. Christians and Jews can read a passage from the Bible each week, and reflect upon what that passage means in their own lives. Take some time together to talk about what religion means to you, and the joys and struggles that you've faced that week. You'll learn about your friends' beliefs as well as your own, and you'll find strength in the week ahead.

Fun on a Dime (or a Penny)

Whether your fresh, unlined face is the result of youth or Botox, you and your girlfriends don't have to spend your life savings having fun together. Sure, you can head off to the casinos, the boutiques, or the spa, but there are plenty of ways to have laughs without breaking the bank. We've always made do in the South, either because we've had to, or because we're smart with our money.

- Don't want to spend thousands of dollars at the spa? Get a facial at home. You can make your own facials with oatmeal and water or cornmeal and water (for exfoliating), avocado (for moisturizing), or cucumber and yogurt (for stressed skin). You might feel funny putting your food on your face, but I say better your face than your thighs! If you're really daring, you can even dye each other's hair but, personally, I wouldn't trust my beautiful tresses to an at-home product.

- Flea markets. Scouring the flea markets with your girlfriends, you'll find a lot of junk and a few treasures, but most of all, you'll have a lot of fun.

- Learn a new hobby together. Taking a sewing, quilting, knitting, or pottery class is usually inexpensive, especially if you search out local community centers and adult continuing education classes. You'll preserve the Southern tradition of making handcrafted goods and, more importantly, you and your girlfriend can bond over your lopsided sweaters and not-quite-even pots.

- Southerners, male and female, love sports. Watch your favorite team at home or at the stadium. And I'm not just talking about the local pro football team. Why not check out the local women's soccer team or the club field hockey team for a change?

We Southern ladies love to play the field: the soccer field, the volleyball court, and the softball field, of course! Gone are the days of the belle lying on the couch in the afternoon. Girls these days know that there's much more fun to be had out in that beautiful Southern sunlight. We could jog or swim by ourselves, but we'd much prefer playing with our girlfriends. The more GRITS on our team, the better. If we're on the tennis court, make it doubles!

WELL, I DECLARE

Sports don't just teach competition; they teach a true Southern virtue: graciousness. U.S. swimmer Aaron Piersol finished a full two seconds ahead of his competitor and friend, Austrian Marcus Rogan. Although the judges initially said that Piersol was disqualified on a very technical point, they reversed their decision before the medal ceremony. Rogan showed true graciousness: "Aaron is a very honest person. I'm sure he swam fairly. For a moment I thought about gold and the idea was just beautiful but, after all, it's fair like this." His friendship with Piersol was more important to him than winning a medal, even an Olympic gold. He went on to say: "No medal is as beautiful as friendship."

For many years, I taught a girls' volleyball team, and I look back fondly at all the girls I knew and loved during that time. Those girls grew stronger mentally and physically by playing together. For some people, sports are about competition, but for the girls I taught, playing with their GRITS friends was as much fun as winning the game. I loved those girls, and it was for them that I made my first "GRITS: Girls Raised in the South" T-shirts. I wanted them to know what truly special young women they were, and in some ways, I think I learned to love myself a bit more in the process.

WELL, I DECLARE

Sports aren't just a great way for girls to have fun with their friends. The Institute for Athletics and Education has found that girls who participate in sports are three times more likely to graduate from high school, eighty percent less likely to have an unwanted pregnancy, and ninety-two percent less likely to use drugs than girls who do not play sports. A Southern parent who teaches a daughter to play sports is giving her a wonderful gift.

A Girl Who Glistened

It shouldn't surprise anyone that the woman who is widely recognized as one of the greatest athletes of the twentieth century is a Southern girl. Mildred Didrikson Zaharias, or "Babe," as she liked to be called, in honor of Babe Ruth, was born in Port Arthur, Texas, in 1914. From an early age, she played sports, and she excelled at everything: softball, basketball, track, and golf. She could play, and she could win.

At the 1932 Olympics in Los Angeles, Didrikson won gold medals in the javelin and 80-meter hurdles and a silver medal for the high jump. She set one world record in the hurdles and tied the record in her other events. When she took up golf, she immediately excelled at that, too. In 1946, she began a string of consecutive tournament wins that has yet to be beaten by anyone, male or female. She later helped organize the Ladies Professional Golf Association (LPGA) to help the sport gain popularity among women.

Although she was diagnosed with cancer in the early 1950s, she continued to play golf, and even after surgery, she continued to win tournaments. She died in 1956 in Galveston, and the courage that she exhibited during her illness showed that she was a winner on and off the field.

A Silk Purse From a Pig's Ear

Making Your Own Breeze

- Sometimes, your friend may seem so down that she'll never get up. She may wake up one morning to discover that her husband hasn't given her a gift more romantic than a bucket of chicken in years, her boss is the young puppy that she trained for the job five years ago, and she weighs the same as the latest heavyweight boxing champ. When you try to bring some fun into her life, all she can do is whine about how rotten her life is. If she resists your offers, don't give up on her. Even under all that sulking and pouting, there's a GRITS who's happy to have your listening ear. Give her time—and keep telling those corny old jokes—and soon she'll realize that life isn't so bad after all with her Southern girlfriends by her side.

- Do you want to be Ginger Rogers, but the man in your life would rather be a couch potato? Dance with your girlfriends. Let your GRITS girlfriend be your partner, and take that dance class you always wanted to. Once you learn the skills, go dancing with a girl by your side; it doesn't matter who leads, as long as you both can remember where your feet are.

You may find male partners, or you may just have each other. Either way, you'll be dancing the night away with a friend.

- If you want to make the average teenage daughter blush down to her toes, all you have to do is be a mother. She may say that she can't face leaving the house as you don your gorgeous red hat, complete with a nest of stuffed cardinals and miles of red netting, to meet with the other ladies. She may absolutely swoon with shame to see you enter the talent show at church. She may think that her life is ruined forever when she sees you selling your fashion creations at the Christmas bazaar. Ignore her, and live your life to the fullest. With time, even the most eye-rolling teenager will realize that her mother is a special person, and she'll be glad that you took the time to live life, rather than hiding in the shadows.

- Just because you've put on a couple of extra pounds over the years doesn't mean you can't get active with your friends. Many times, women are afraid to get out there and shake their bodies just because of a little extra jiggle. Your girlfriends won't mind hitting around a tennis ball or jogging through the neighborhood with you just because you aren't supermodel-thin; in fact, they'll prefer getting active with a woman with a real woman's body. Go ahead and squeeze yourself into your old sports clothes—or, better yet, grab your girlfriends and shop for something new and flattering—and get glistening. Your friends will love having you along, and your body will thank you.

CHAPTER 7

What a Trip

"He who would travel happily must travel light."
—ANTOINE DE SAINT-EXUPÉRY
(Honey, he obviously never traveled with a Southern girl!)

"Through travel I first became aware of the outside world; it was through travel that I found my own introspective way into becoming a part of it."
—EUDORA WELTY, MISSISSIPPI

Whether we're crossing the country in a new convertible or just heading down to the mall in an old Buick, if there's one thing we GRITS like better than being in our own town with our girlfriends, it's getting out and seeing someone else's. We love getting out, Thelma and Louise–style, at least until we get to the part about driving over a cliff—we might be fun, sugar, but we're not stupid.

PEARL OF WISDOM

"Thelma, this is some vacation."
—Louise, Thelma and Louise

GRITS Don't Pack Light

When we hit the road, GRITS know that the most important thing to take along is your girlfriend! When trying to figure out how you can fit everything you need for a weekend trip into twelve suitcases, remember to bring a few of these along:

- *Your own hair dryer. Sure, even highway motels often have hair dryers these days, but they're usually low-power and* low-quality. Southern belles wouldn't dream of hitting the road with damp, frizzy hair, so bring a hair dryer that can handle your gorgeous tresses.

- Water. Driving with the top down can take its toll on your skin, and the dust can get in your throat. Stay hydrated.

- Healthy snacks. Road food too often means burgers, barbecue, and, for some of us, bourbon. A steady diet of salt, fat, and sugar can take its toll on your mood, your skin, and your body. Pack fresh and dried fruit, rice cakes, whole-grain crackers, ziplock bags of veggies, small boxes of cereal, and other foods that can keep you energized without ruining your waistline.

- Music. When you're out in the middle of nowhere, and the radio offers you the choice of the farm report and German opera, you'll be glad you packed those tapes or CDs. Songs that you can sing along to at the top of your lungs are great, and songs that bring back good memories of your times together are better yet.

- Phone numbers. GRITS seem to know someone just about everywhere they go. Don't miss the opportunity to reconnect with your second cousin twice removed, or your old roommate from college. Someone who knows the area can point you to those fabulous spots that only the locals seem to know and, if you're invited, sleeping in the guest room is a lot more personal, and cheaper, than a roadside motel.

PEARL OF WISDOM

"I love you more than my luggage."
—Steel Magnolias

GRITS GLOSSARY

Shag [shag] n. *1. A dance made popular in Myrtle Beach, South Carolina, during the 1950s, and still a great reason to jump into the car and dance the night away. 2. A type of carpet no self-respecting GRITS girl would have in her house. 3. In British English, something that no well-bred Southern girl would discuss in public!*

In college, my girlfriends and I took road trips. As a newlywed, and later a young mother, we took beach trips and shopping trips. Later, when the children were in college, we made the most of visiting our children together. Now that most of my friends' children are out on their own, we do whatever we want! Our friendship has been about moving from one stage in our lives to another and, sugah, the trip has sure been sweet.

PEARL OF WISDOM

After a few days in the same car, sometimes even Southern girls can get into each other's perfectly coiffed hair. At least once a day, try to spend some time by yourself: take a soak in the hotel hot tub, a long walk to stretch your legs, or just go out for a coffee on your own. As sparkling as your personality is, it's nice to give your girlfriend a little time for herself as well. The time you spend back in the car with your girlfriends will be all the more fun for the time you take for yourself.

These days, a lot of Southern girls could fly off to Cancún or London if they chose, but there's nothing that's quite the same as getting behind the wheel with your girlfriends.

You can take the back roads and see what the South is really like once you get off the interstate. You can flirt with those cute men in the next booth at the diner or the next spot on the campground. You can play silly games counting license plates or cows. You can battle with the wind to set up your tent or, better yet, just plunk down your credit card for a room with those staples of Southern female life, the air conditioner and hair dryer. You can spend hours chatting about everything from your kids to your favorite *American Idol* star. You can sing at the top of your lungs to the radio.

PEARL OF WISDOM

Whatever you do, don't let someone convince you to hide from the world. The husband of one GRITS I know told her she couldn't go on a cruise with her girlfriends because she was too old and fat. She not only went on the cruise, she went parasailing. And she's going back next year. That's the GRITS attitude!

WELL, I DECLARE

When I think of reckless young drivers, I think of teenage boys, but it turns out I may be wrong. A recent survey found that while fifty-six percent of women between the ages of eighteen and twenty-four believe that it's acceptable to travel ten miles an hour over the speed limit on highways, only forty-six percent of males do. Seems those pretty little heels have some lead in them!

So Many Places, So Little Time

If you even bother having a destination, you've got all the South to choose from: the best golf courses in the country, if not the world, windy mountain roads, gracious mansions, sweet jazz rhythms, soft sands, and rollicking parties. While our cities have style, our charming small towns are proud to welcome you as guests. There's as much variety in places to stop in the South as there is in us Southern girls.

- **Beaufort, South Carolina:** *While down the road in Hilton Head golfers tee up and diners dress to the nines, in relaxed Beaufort, time seems to stand still. Wander the streets and see gracious mansions or the homey main street before too many Hollywood stars buy the homes and bring in the tourists.*
- **Lakeland, Florida:** *When people think of Frank Lloyd Wright, few think of central Florida, but the most famous of American architects designed several buildings at Florida Southern College. Lakeland is about an hour's drive from Orlando, so when you're tired of the Mouse and want a bit of culture instead, drive on down the road to Lakeland.*
- **Natchez Trace Parkway:** *This lovely stretch of road begins in Natchez, Mississippi, and runs to a point near Nashville, Tennessee. The Trace runs roughly along ancient Native American paths and is run by the National Park Service. There are plenty of historic sites, visitor centers, and interpretive centers along the way, so you won't be cooped up in the car for the entire four-hundred-plus miles.*
- **Rock City, Georgia:** *Countless country road signs couldn't be wrong. Near the northern border of Georgia, this tourist attraction is one of the best-advertised in the South. A spectacular natural setting, where it's rumored you can see*

five states on a clear day, combines with some less-than-spectacular tourist displays, such as Fairyland Caverns and Mother Goose Village, to create a classic Southern tourist trap.

- **San Antonio, Texas:** *San Antonio has pieces of Texas's Spanish past and its modern present. Visit the Alamo, stroll down the River Walk, or catch some art (and air-conditioning) in one of its museums.*
- **Wetumpka, Alabama:** *A gem of a town whose setting on a beautiful river has brought several filmmakers to town.*

Part of the fun of a road trip is that you don't have to be yourself when you're on the road. Being a GRITS, you will always act like a lady, but it's a chance to do things you'd never do otherwise. It's an opportunity for a hardworking accountant to play a round of mini golf just like a kid. A housewife can dress to the nines and eat at a restaurant where the food isn't served from plastic. A teetotaler can take a few sips of piña colada. A great-grandmother can throw on a tropical print bathing suit and strut her stuff down the shore. A marathoner can sleep late and take a few nibbles of fudge. Acting crazy is all the more fun since you'll have your girlfriends at your side to egg you on.

See You Next Week, Same Time, Same Place

Vicki Miller was so tickled by her mother's travels that she just had to share her story with me. Alia Czarneski of Cookville, Tennessee, travels regularly with her girlfriends, even though they never leave their town. She and her four friends share breakfast every Monday morning at a local café. Thursday is the day they have their hair done, and catch up on the week's gossip, of course, at the local beauty school. Saturday means cappuccino at the local truck stop. When Saturday night rolls around, you can find these friends eating barbecue together. Times, places, and food never change. Even the number of the group—five—is always the same. If a member of the group moves away or passes on, Alia and her friends have to search for a replacement!

A Silk Purse From a Pig's Ear

Trips Without Trauma

To avoid being stranded by the side of the road in the middle of the night, soaking wet from a spring thunderstorm, and threatening to scratch each other's eyes out, take a few simple precautions.

- Keep the trip short but sweet. While an epic cross-country road trip might seem great in theory, when you've seen the thousandth cornfield the Midwest has to offer, the front seat is molded into the shape of your backside, your spine has compacted into your tailbone, and you've discussed your friend's marital problems for three days running, you may regret ever pulling out of your driveway. Manageable trips let you have fun with your girlfriends, and they keep the excitement going. Believe it or not, you can have too much of a good thing.

- Plan something to look forward to each day. When the day is hot, the air conditioner is on the fritz, and every mile of road is starting to look the same, it's important to have a highlight to keep you positive. Whether it's the best mutton barbecue in the state of Kentucky, the world's largest chair in North Carolina, or women swimming around dressed as mermaids in Florida, something to get excited about will keep your trip going strong.

- Have a trusted mechanic check out your car before you leave. You don't want to be five hundred miles from home when you discover that your transmission (whatever that does) needs a complete overhaul. In case he (or she!) misses something, make sure your AAA membership is up-to-date.

- Jumper cables. Even if you don't know what connects where, you can bet that a nice businessman on his way home from work does, and he'll be more than happy to help out a carful of lovely GRITS.

- Pack a cell phone. Some GRITS detest cell phones. They see the man walking down the sidewalk and talking loudly about his vasectomy for all to hear, the teenage girl discussing her boyfriend during the best part of the movie, the woman weaving through traffic with a cigarette in one hand, the phone in the other, and they vow never to get the hated thing. I think those women would think differently when they have two flat tires in the middle of a rainstorm, and they're thirty miles from nowhere. If you're a GRITS, you won't let a phone excuse rude behavior, but you will have a lifeline if something goes wrong on your trip.

CHAPTER 8

Southern Clubs and Disorganizations

"When I am an old woman, I shall wear purple/With a red hat that doesn't go, and doesn't suit me . . . And make up for the sobriety of my youth."—JENNY JOSEPH

"If the first woman God ever made was strong enough to turn the world upside down, these women together ought to be able to turn it right side up again."—SOJOURNER TRUTH

I f having one GRITS for a girlfriend is wonderful, imagine having a whole group of them. If the men in our lives think that we're nothing but a group of old hens, well, that's fine with us; then they won't try to crash our meetings. Whether we're Instant GRITS going to our first scout meetings, college girls passing the candle at a sorority initiation, or Sweet Potato Queens strutting in our sequins and heels, we love surrounding ourselves with the women we love.

Southern women get together just to have fun, and they get together for important causes. We don't need minutes or a meeting hall; a couple of women and a common cause is all we need to change the world.

The Ladies of the Club

- *Clubs and organizations can give your daughter the kind of positive peer pressure that can turn her into the lady you know is there under the gum-chewing and the ratty old jeans. Encourage her to join the Girl Scouts (founded by a true Southern lady, Juliette Gordon Lowe), a sports team, or one of her school's clubs. She may miss her afternoon soaps at first,*

*but soon she'll look forward to spending her days with the
wonderful GRITS she calls her friends.*

- *You don't have to be a member of an elite country club to be
surrounded by ladies. It isn't money or connections that make
a woman into a lady; it's the way that she behaves and treats
others. Your local women's or garden club can be just as much
fun, and a lot less expensive. In my opinion, any organization
with GRITS as members is the place to be seen.*

- *If you're far away from home, nothing can ease your
homesickness like the sweet, soft voices of the South. Groups of
native Southerners exist even in the most frigid Northern
climes, so check your local bulletin board, the Internet or, the
best source of all, another local Southerner, to find out where
they meet.*

- *While the image many of us have of Southern clubs is limited
to ladies in white gloves sipping tea, or sorority girls with
perfect hair, Southern women come in all shapes and sizes.
Volunteer and charitable organizations, groups of women
sharing their hobbies, and religious organizations exist
throughout the South. If we Southern ladies all shared the
same interests (other than men and hair, of course—those are
our birthrights) we'd all be pretty boring.*

SOS: Sisters of Sororities

If anything shows how much Southern college women value
their friendships, it's their commitment to sororities. For a
Southern girl, a sorority is not an extracurricular activity; it's
serious work, the center of her college career, and friends for
life. From the time she enters college, and often when she's still

in high school, GRITS are planning for Rush Week. After all, it is never, ever too soon to start thinking about which three letters are going to define your life for the next four years.

WELL, I DECLARE

When people talk about "Southern" sororities, they usually mean sororities that are especially active in the South. The fact is that many well-known sororities began in the Southern states. Alpha Delta Pi and Phi Mu were both founded at Wesleyan Female College in Macon, Georgia, in the 1850s. Alpha Kappa Alpha was founded at Howard University in Washington, D.C. Chi Omega has its origins in Arkansas. Kappa Delta hails from Virginia. Just like their wonderful GRITS members, these sororities are daughters of the South.

Sorority life begins with "Rush," the process by which sororities recruit new members, and drive themselves, and their rushees, crazy. Almost-grown women spend days building decorations out of papier mâché to attract women who will be their sisters for the next several years. Every school is different, of course, but essentially Rush is a series of parties where recruits get to know the sororities and sororities get to know the recruits. It sounds, and feels, an awful lot like dating, but there aren't any pesky men around.

The first parties are usually short and informal, then build up to more fancy-dress, longer parties. Rush consumes the lives of college women, at least for a couple of weeks. It's a time for hand-wringing and tears for Southern women (and their mothers, of course), but it's all worth it in the end because this isn't just about a house to live in, it's about finding the women you want to be friends with for the rest of your life.

PEARL OF WISDOM

When choosing your outfit for Rush, remember that you're out to win the hearts of women, not the eyes of men. While you should always be attractive, you should also look like a lady. A simple and elegant dress is always better than a plunging back or neckline, and simple jewelry, such as a strand of pearls or a simple choker, is preferable to anything dangling or showy.

GRITS GLOSSARY

Legacy [le gə see] n. *The daughter, niece, sister, or cousin of a present or former sorority member. Although some say that any legacy with a pulse will receive a bid (an invitation to join), legacy status usually does not guarantee membership. Even the great-granddaughter of your founder can't show up to a rush event in dirty overalls and a Mohawk, unless, of course, the party theme is punk tractor pull.*

After getting a bid, a sorority girl faces initiation. Now, she might have heard tales of blood oaths or secrets that she cannot divulge on pain or death. The fact is, though no sorority woman worth her pin will divulge the initiation rites, expect to walk around the room blindfolded a couple of times and maybe say a couple of oaths in high-falutin language. Fraternity boys may tell pledges that they have to jump off a wall blindfolded (even if that wall turns out to be six inches off the ground), and force their pledges to run naked through town, but most sororities are just too ladylike to do that kind of thing. Let's face it, college boys have no more sense than a pack of drunken monkeys. Sorority girls might ask their pledges to have shaving cream fights or wear silly outfits, but they're not going to torture their sisters, for goodness sakes.

Now, some men might tell you that sorority life is about scantily-clad women having pillow fights. Honey, if you believe that, you've watched one too many teen movies. Sororities are about sisterhood, and they're about making a difference in the community. Every sorority sister gives hours each semester volunteering for the sorority's official charity, as well as university and community events and other charities near to the sisters' hearts. Sorority sisters sell candy, calendars and, of course, kisses, to raise money. They work with children, the sick, and the elderly. They clean up parks and highways. Southern sorority sisters put in all this work because they love taking care of other people, but they also do it because they love their sisters. Let's face it: Women willing to chip their nails for their friends are sisters indeed!

WELL, I DECLARE

Although some people, Northerners I suspect, have suggested that sorority girls are somehow less intelligent or serious than independents, studies have shown that sorority members actually have higher grade point averages than non-sorority members.

After all that work, sorority sisters love to get together and act like the sisters they are. They make party decorations out of nothing but chicken wire and old newspapers. They put together baskets of goodies for new pledges or children they're tutoring. They work up a sweat in group jogging or aerobics. They make late-night trips to the bowling alley or the diner. They pile into a car to take over Panama City. Of course, they also have to learn every word of their sorority songs. Some sorority songs are serious, some are silly, and some, well . . . let's just say I won't print the lyrics to "Take a Chi Phi in the Corner" in this book. But I guarantee if you're a AEPi you know the exact words I'm talking about.

PEARL OF WISDOM

Some Southern girls love primping and preening for sorority formals, but some of us would much rather throw on a pair of blue jeans and play Frisbee on the quad. When you or your daughter are selecting a sorority, keep in mind that each has a different character. If your idea of going all-out on makeup is a quick coat of lip gloss, you probably won't be comfortable in a sorority full of perfectly coiffed blondes. For every sorority that emphasizes the looks of its sisters, there are more that emphasize friendship, community service, and learning. Go with the sorority that makes you happy, not the one that is the most prestigious, and you'll find that your college experience is much more rewarding.

One of the greatest parts of being in a sorority is meeting those fraternity boys. Sororities get together for informal parties, mixers, and formal dances. Let's face it, a Kappa Alpha just wouldn't be the same without his "sunny Southern sweetheart," his "Kappa Alpha rose." Crying over a boy, both for love and hate, makes female friendship all the sweeter.

GRITS GLOSSARY

Lavaliere [la və lir] n. *A charm with Greek letters symbolizing a sorority or a fraternity. When a brother gives a woman his lavaliere, it's a symbol of his commitment to ask her to fetch him beer for the rest of his life.*

No matter how much a Southern girl looks forward to the day when she gets a pin or a lavaliere from her Southern fraternity man, that moment is not as sweet as the day she gets a bid from her sisters. We love having a commitment from a boy, but going through a candle ceremony with our girlfriends afterward is even better. Boyfriends are wonderful, but our girlfriends are friends for life.

WELL, I DECLARE

There's a rumor that an astronaut left a Tri-Delt pin behind on the moon in honor of his favorite Southern girl. True or not, the story shows how much Southern women treasure their sororities, and how much Southern men treasure their Southern sorority girls.

You Got Your Grits in My Sweet Potatoes . . . Red Hats, Ya-Yas, and More

Southern women like to get together to work, to grow, and to love their girlfriends, but they also get together to celebrate the fact that they're Southern. We might have been blessed to be born in the greatest part of this beautiful country, we might have adopted it as our new home, or we might be living far away, longing for a taste of home. Whatever the reason, sometimes we Southern girls love to get together and hear those sweet voices that are truly the song of the South. We know that our girlfriends are fabulous, even if they'd blush to hear us say it, so getting together for no other reason than enjoying our Southern sisters is sometimes the best reason of all.

Red Hot Hatters

One of the most popular organizations (or "disorganizations," as the founder likes to call it) is the Red Hat Society. Red Hatters know that just because we've made it to the good side of fifty doesn't mean we can't gather to have fun with our girlfriends. In fact, I think we can have more fun. The Red Hats are not strictly Southern, but in their love of life and their spirit, I think that they embody a lot of what is good in the South. The only requirement to join is that there are no requirements, other than to wear a red hat and have fun. There are thousands of Red Hat groups all over the country. Here's just a sample of the Southern groups (from The Red Hat Society *by Sue Ellen Cooper):*

Red Hat Hot Flashers	Atlanta, Georgia
The Grateful Red	Bonita Springs, Florida
Sophisticated Seniors of the Scarlet Chapeau	Birmingham, Alabama
Bootin' Scootin Red Bonnets	Dallas, Texas
Goddess (Gorgeous Old Dames Doing Estrogen Someday Soon)	Dallas, Texas

Red Hot Mental Pausers	Griffin, Georgia
Razorback Red Hats	Hot Springs, Arkansas
Red Hat Chili Mamas	Jackson, Mississippi
Bluegrass ThoroughREDS	Lexington, Kentucky
Still Magnolias	Natchitoches, Mississippi
Scarlet O'Hatters of Pawley's Island	Pawley's Island, South Carolina
Divine Sirens of the Ha Ha Sisterhood	Raleigh, North Carolina

PEARL OF WISDOM

"There is fun after fifty for women of all walks of life—who believe that silliness is the comic relief of life. Since we're all in this together, we might as well join red-gloved hands together. Underneath the frivolity, we share a bond of affection forged by common life experiences and genuine enthusiasm for wherever life takes us."—Sue Ellen Cooper, Queen Mother of the Red Hat Society

Classy Lassies

The Classy Lassies of Muscle Shoals, Alabama, are Southern ladies from the tips of our perfectly styled hair to our well-pedicured toes. We entered the first annual City of Muscle Shoals Christmas Parade and carried it off in style. The ladies had sewing parties to make gorgeous matching outfits, complete with red hats and muffs. We crafted a float complete with a miniature house, sleigh, and horse. Our float even included a tree decorated with adorable little red hats.

On the way to the parade, however, our troubles began. High winds blew the house off the truck and onto a nearby field. Some passersby, being kind Southerners, rescued our house, but only a portion survived. Thank goodness some of our menfolk arrived with hammers and nails to salvage it before the parade began. Then, right before the judges arrived, the lights on our tree went out. One of our innovative ladies politely asked a nearby store owner to loan us an extension cord, and we hooked the lights up to a cigarette lighter in the car towing our float.

A bit of Southern ingenuity saved the day. We ended up winning best float, and no one got pneumonia. Best of all, we had a great time, just like the Classy Lassies that we are!

—Joan Marsh
Alabama

WELL, I DECLARE

The Junior League, an organization of women that seeks to aid local communities, has chapters throughout the South, and elite society women are often attracted to the organization. It might come as a surprise, then, that it was a debutante from—of all places—New York City who founded the organization. It just goes to show that you can find GRITS in the most unexpected places!

These days, it seems like women all over the South are starting Southern clubs. Some women get together to celebrate being natives of a state or city, some to be Ya-Yas, Sweet Potatoes, Red Hats, or (I'm blushing) GRITS together. With our world changing so fast, and with so many newcomers in our midst, we GRITS are sometimes afraid that the South is losing its character. Women miss the days when they were surrounded by the voices of their Southern sisters. As many wonderful changes as there have been in the South, there are also wonderful traditions worth preserving. By forming these clubs, GRITS can help preserve some of what makes the South so special, and they can get together with their wonderful GRITS sisters in the process.

WELL, I DECLARE

Most days of the year, New York is full of brawls, but one day each summer, it's full of drawls. For twenty-five years, Mississippi natives have been gathering in New York's Central Park to share Southern food, talk, and friendship. This annual summer get-together helps native Southerners keep a little bit of home, a little bit of sanity, and a little bit of real Southern barbecue in the city that never sleeps.

A Southern Girl in Michigan

Living in Michigan, I can't count the times I longed for a little bit of home. My salvation was when I met my Southern girlfriends. I cannot explain to anyone who is not from the South what it is to hear a drawl and know the difference between Birmingham and Montgomery. My husband adores seeing me light up when I hear the incredible melody of a Southern voice; I feel a warmth all over when I hear a Southern lady or gentleman speaking.

When my Southern girlfriends get together, the only agenda is no agenda. We show up, talk Southern, and ask, "Who are your peo-

ple?" We discuss the tragedy of lack of manners and openness, and we talk about the cultural differences between Michigan and the land we miss and hold so dear to our hearts.

Sometimes, I'm not certain those wonderful Ya-Yas down in Baldwin County and Houston fully appreciate what they have. Remember us up here in the frigid Midwest, and count your blessings!

—Martha Jane Thompson
Michigan

A Friend in Need Is a Friend Indeed

Southerners have a long history of standing by their neighbors in times of need. Whether it meant feeding the children of a family that had been out of work for a while, helping to patch up a neighbor's roof when a tornado hit town, or donating to the local church, we Southerners could not have survived without giving to our neighbors.

Southern women carry on this tradition of giving back today through numerous service organizations. Whether they're teenagers active in a service organization, retired women helping out a local hospital, or homemakers who host parties to raise funds for a charity, Southern women give back to their communities. They serve to make their hometowns better places to live; they serve to spend time with their girlfriends; and they serve because they care. I'd like to think that they serve because, to Southerners, we're all one big extended family, so helping others is really a way of helping ourselves.

PEARL OF WISDOM

"The fragrance always remains on the hand that gives the rose."
—Mahatma Gandhi

Getting involved is easy. Share your special gifts, and you'll find that not only do you make new friends, but you feel that you have a greater purpose in life. A lawyer can represent not only her wealthy clients, but a pro bono defendant. A seamstress can sew not only for her own family or her customers, but for a local drama troupe. A baker can fatten up her own husband, and she can donate her scrumptious goodies to the school or church bake sale. Even if you don't feel that you have a special talent, a willing pair of hands can be useful. If you can't install a roof or put up drywall for Habitat for Humanity (a Southern organization, naturally), you can always bring lunch to those who can, and when you do, you might find yourself eating beside a wonderful new girlfriend. And if she can help you remodel your bathroom, honey, even better!

From Yellow Dog Democrats to the GOP (Grand Old Parties, that is!)

For a lot of our history, politics in the South has been a game that the boys kept to themselves. Now, Southern girls are joining an elite club themselves, and making a career in politics. Southern women have been slowly moving into politics, and they're trying to teach those boys a thing or two. Southern women are naturals at politics. We love to meet new people, we could make conversation with a tree stump, and everybody loves us, or at least everyone with taste. We know when to talk and when to keep our mouths shut, and our mothers taught us to respect everyone, even if they are wrong about everything.

WELL, I DECLARE

Of the thirty-six states that ratified the Nineteenth Amendment, granting women the right to vote, only four were in the South. Down here in the South, though, we weren't all against women entering political life: The first woman to serve as a U.S. Senator was Latimer Felton, a Georgia Democrat.

We Southern girls learn politics from our mothers and our friends. Now, I don't mean that we argue about taxes and school vouchers at dinner parties; ladies know that politics doesn't make suitable evening conversation. I'm talking practical politics, by which I mean the art of keeping everyone, even cranky old Aunt Melinda, the one who always smells a little bit like cats, smiling. We aren't arrogant, and we don't puff ourselves up; we just practice the art of making others happy. We know how to play being the belle of the ball without making anyone else feel like a wallflower. We know how to make every single man at a party feel that he's the center of our attention. We know how to balance filling the buffet table, making conversation with shy guests, and keeping the teenagers away from the bar, and we can do it all with a smile on our faces. We aren't born belles; we learn from watching our mother, sisters, and friends. With all the amazing women we've learned from, juggling constituents and special interests should be no problem for a skilled GRITS.

WELL, I DECLARE

Women in politics aren't just elected to office; sometimes they work behind the scenes. When Barbara and George Bush married, Barbara started keeping information about their new friends on note cards. She listed names of family members, birthdays, and if she had them over for a meal, she added what was served along with what they liked. When George began his career in politics, everyone was amazed at the wealth of information she had gathered over the years. I understand that the list of friends she had was invaluable to his presidential campaign!

Living with our girlfriends gives us negotiating skills no Harvard business graduate can match. Southern girls are beautiful and charming, but every once in a while, we can be just the teeniest touch high-maintenance. We need counter space for our hot rollers and mirror space to put our faces on. Honey, it takes time to look like a true Southern lady, and anyone who's negotiated bathroom use between two or three Southern sisters or roommates knows the meaning of the word "diplomacy." Getting a public works project for our district is nothing next to getting Mavis away from the makeup mirror without breaking a nail!

A GRITS Politician

Elizabeth Dole, or Liddy to her friends, is a Salisbury, North Carolina, native and a political natural. At Duke University, Liddy served as student body president. She served in various capacities under Presidents Nixon, Reagan, and Bush. Later, she continued her life in public service as president of the American Red Cross. In 2002, she was elected to the office of senator serving North Carolina.

Liddy Dole looks and behaves every inch the Southern lady. Like any good Southern lady, she has been a loyal and supportive wife to her husband Robert Dole, a former Senator and U.S. presidential candidate. As strong and successful as she has been, Elizabeth Dole is every inch a GRITS friend, and no matter what happens, she can still count on her Tri-Delt sisters to vote for her at the polls.

A Silk Purse From a Pig's Ear

Club Flubs

- Countless Southern mothers have received the dreaded call from her daughter in college; her favorite sorority hasn't come through with a bid or, worse yet, no sorority has asked her to be a sister. Listen to her tears, even if it seems like a small problem to you; to her, it's a tragedy, and that's what matters. Let her know that everything will be all right, and that you'll be there for her. She needs a shoulder to cry on. Time—and all the excitement she'll find in college life—will heal her wounds.
- Even some of us Southern girls would rather strike out on our own than join together with our girlfriends. Southerners have

always had an independent spirit. If you're one of these, you're no less Southern, and the same goes for your daughters and granddaughters who'd rather walk on their own than step with the herd. When you receive an invitation to join a club or other organization—and you surely will, Southerners being the welcoming types that they are—politely begging off the invitation is acceptable. Better yet, tell your friend that you'd love to meet her for lunch or coffee, where you can spend time just getting to know her better, but that you aren't much interested in being a part of a large group.

- Some existing organizations have difficulty bringing in new members. The members might be friendly on their own, but they've grown comfortable together, and they don't fancy working a newcomer into the existing routine. If you're still interested in joining, give the old members time to make you welcome; soon, you may find yourself part of that comfortable circle. If you're still uncomfortable, don't feel bad about walking away. A club that doesn't want a GRITS is not a club worth joining.

CHAPTER 9

Living Southern Style

"You don't need a certain number of friends, only a number of friends you can be certain of."—PATTI LABELLE, *Pennsylvania* (*but we still love her, sugah*)

"Do not ever give a Queen a home appliance as a gift. Period. The End."—JILL CONNER BROWN, *THE SWEET POTATO QUEENS' BOOK OF LOVE*

Picture a Southern belle lounging on her front porch, not a care in the world other than which beau she's going to dance with first. In the movies, she'd waltz into the next scene, floating on a cloud of silk and charm. In the real world, she'd have to wrestle with the bank for another extension on her mortgage payment, iron and starch each one of those petticoats, and chase those no-good cousins and their firecrackers out from under the front porch steps. Even so, she'd always have a calm, welcoming smile on her face.

Since GRITS live in the real world, they know what it is to struggle, to face down problems from bad marriages to faulty plumbing. GRITS manage to live through their problems with their friends at their sides. Though sometimes we feel like we can't handle one more challenge, that one more call from our son's principal or one more "past due" notice will send us over the edge, our friends manage to drag us through. Life is full of obstacles, but our friends point out to us that it is also full of joys.

The Martha Stewarts of the world might tell us that living is about baking the perfect cake and setting the perfect table. We Southern girls can do those things, of course, but we know that living is about so much more. Living is not about the things we do; it's about the people we love. Friends help us learn, grow, overcome problems, make a home, and just live our lives well.

Add a Pearl, Drop a Pearl

Friends help us every minute of our lives, whether they're going out of their way to help us, or they're just in the background, giving us their silent support. Take a moment to give them something back, and let them know how much they mean to you.

- *If a friend's parents are in a nursing home, take a few moments to visit them. Your friends—and their parents—will be grateful that you took the time to brighten their day.*
- *Send your friends' children a card for birthdays, graduations, or just to say hello. A college boy or girl won't want to admit how much they miss home, but your card will be welcomed.*
- *Collect photos that your friend will love—of her children, her pets, her friends—and send them to her as a surprise.*
- *Bake her a cake or her favorite pie for no reason other than letting her know you care. Anybody can give a birthday cake; it's the any-old-day cake that really shows you love her. And don't forget to offer to come over and share.*
- *Send your friend newspaper clippings or magazine articles that might interest her, especially if she's moved far away.*
- *Make a donation in her honor to her favorite charity.*
- *Give your friend a new address book, complete with updated addresses of all your mutual friends, as well as other helpful numbers, such as the mechanic and pizza delivery place. And, honey, I don't have to tell a Southern girl that the number to the liposuction clinic won't be appreciated, no matter how much it's needed.*

Not all work takes place in an office. Whether they're full-time homemakers or working the "second shift," any Southern woman can tell you that some of the toughest and most rewarding labor takes place in her own home. Working with their hands has always been a part of Southern women's lives. Our grandmothers would turn bits of old cloth into comfortable quilts to get their children through the winter. They would smoke their own hams, can their own pickles, and even brew their own hard cider to feed their families long after the hogs were slaughtered and the crops harvested. From wealthy plantation women who decorated their homes in their own needlepoint to poor tenant farmers who worked the fields along with their husbands, the domestic arts were part of every Southern woman's life.

Even when the domestic arts were about simple survival, they were also about friendship. Making soap, mending clothes, and canning peaches are skills that take years to perfect, and sometimes require at least two strong backs and two sets of hands, and a mother or friends were always there to teach the household secrets. Goodness, I need a girlfriend to help me find my own kitchen; I can't imagine baking my own bread each day from scratch, including cutting the wood to feed the stove, and sewing every dress on my daughters' backs without someone to help me and ease the way. Sure, Southern women still bake their own biscuits, but that's nothing compared to the sort of back-breaking labor that used to go into simple survival. Women stood by each other to make sure that the strawberries jelled, the stitches were tight and straight, and the rows in the garden were straight and weeded. The labor went faster with laughter and talk to smooth it along.

Domestic work was not just a method of surviving; it was a method of self-expression. Harriet Powers, who was born a slave in Georgia, used her quilts to tell stories. Though they were the work of a poor, rural woman, they were nevertheless works of art. Two of her quilts survive and are owned by the Smithsonian American History Museum and the Museum of Fine Arts, Boston.

In some ways, the domestic arts are still about survival for some Southern women; just look at how many make a living selling hand-painted furniture or homemade clothing. I myself used my own hand to make items to sell. I even bought thrift-store fur coats to make unique pillows that were not only as well-made as anything you'd find in a store, but also a lot more interesting. For most of us, though, the domestic arts aren't just about keeping food on the table, they're about preserving our traditions and having fun. From the basic skills to the little tricks of experts, GRITS guide their friends along.

PEARL OF WISDOM

When you're first learning, don't expect everything you make to be perfect. Don't be afraid if your knit cap is a little too big and floppy or your cherry jam is a bit runny; your friends and family will appreciate the work and love that you put into everything you make. And if you stick it out, you'll find that hand-crafted work is finer, and will last longer, than anything you can buy in a department store.

The domestic arts are also about keeping our relationships in a world that is too often about driving on the highway and watching television. When we work beside our girlfriends, we have the time to talk, to rest our minds while our hands are busy working. In a time when doors have locks and cars have loud stereos, when we surround ourselves with things that keep us alone, working together helps bring us together. The work is about creating something unique and preserving our past, but it's also very much about building our relationships with each other.

WELL, I DECLARE

The Southern Highland Crafts Guild is an organization of men and women artists who celebrate the traditional folk arts of people in the mountainous regions of the South. These artists make everything from hand-blown glass to quilts, and their work shows that mountain people aren't just whittling soap on the porch; they're creating beautiful and lasting works of art. To see the traditional and contemporary arts of the region, visit the Folk Art Center or the annual Craft Fair, both in Asheville, North Carolina.

Gritsized

I was born and raised in southern Indiana just the other side of the Gritsline, that imaginary line that separates those who eat grits from the rest of the country. For thirty-nine years now since my marriage, I have been moving back and forth across the Gritsline. One of the ways I've tried to get grits-ed was by joining local pottery groups, but I'm not sure how much that has helped. Once when I asked my older friend in Georgia if she thought I was Southern, she said to me, "You're nice, but you're not Southern."

Recently my husband and I attended a Birmingham formal affair (they do these so well in Gritsland). At our table was a former beauty queen from Tuscaloosa who said to me, "I know you are new here, where did you move from?" I replied "New Jersey." She said in a tone of horror, "Oh no! Well, we have our own ways of doing things in the South. You'll have to learn." Well, I guess she thought maybe she should give me GRITS lessons or something.

Then, a couple of weeks later, I had crossed the Gritsline to go to a wedding in Indiana. I was sitting at the table and a Midwesterner across the table said to me, "Where do you live?" I replied, "Birmingham, Alabama." She said to me in a mocking Southern voice, "Are you one of those Southern belles we hear about?" I didn't tell her that I would just love to be a Southern belle. When you straddle the Gritsline, it seems like you just can't win.

No matter how long I'm south of the Gritsline, I'm sometimes still surprised by the people I meet. One time our pottery class in Georgia was going for a fun weekend to the Fripp Island home of one of the girls. We were going down the interstate nearing Savannah when Reba, a class member about a generation older than the rest of us, said out of the blue: "I've never been away with strangers before." Well, Reba is a fine woman and she had been all over the country, but not with people she knew just from a pottery class. Was this a proper Southern thing to do? she must have been thinking.

I just love that about Reba, and I hope maybe a little bit of her South-of-the-Gritsline charm has rubbed off on me.

—Karin W. Cobb
Alabama

Living together doesn't mean just supporting each other in times of need; it means building a life with our friends and our neighbors. Whether we're just starting out in a studio apartment, or we've made it into that big columned mansion, Southern girls turn to their girlfriends to help with all the skills of making the good life: cooking, gardening and, of course, decorating.

All Southern little girls play house. When I was a little girl, my friends and I would build not only houses, but entire neighborhoods, out of dried cornstalks. It was easy to stack the stalks into neat rows of houses with roads in between. Southern men, on the other hand, are—usually—completely helpless decorators. They're happy with a ratty old armchair, a television to pick up the game, and a fridge with a cold one, and not much else, in it. Why, I knew a young man whose first apartment had nothing but a reclining chair and a big-screen TV, and he thought he was in hog heaven. Southern girls are different; they want even that first apartment to be special.

CRITS GLOSSARY

Hog heaven [hog heəv-n] n. *Home of the Arkansas Razorbacks. (Or, wherevah you're feeling on Cloud Nine!) Woooo pig!*

PEARL OF WISDOM

"Remember that the most valuable antiques are dear old friends."
—H. Jackson Brown

Thank goodness we have such wonderful girlfriends to help us, or we might never get any of those disagreeable chores done! Girlfriends will help you put up a couple of coats of paint to hide those boring white walls or, worse, cover up those strange stains that you wish were white. They'll help you lay down shelf paper to make those kitchen cabinets and drawers feel like your own, even if that kitchen is no bigger than a shoebox. They'll help you scrub down that strange, gunky bathroom until it's something fit for a Southern girl.

Lining the Nest: Tips on Decorating Your First Apartment

- *Don't turn up your nose at hand-me-downs. Raid your family's basements and attics for those pieces that no one else is using.*
- *No matter what your boyfriend says, avoid decorating with anything handed out by a beer company.*
- *If you or your mother sew, make pretty but inexpensive slipcovers to disguise that old Salvation Army couch.*
- *After a quick trip to the hardware store, you can learn to make*

basic repairs yourself. Don't be afraid to ask for help and, besides, it's the perfect excuse to talk to that cute guy in the paint section.

- *If you have the time and can afford cable, watch some of those wonderful decorating shows on television, or dig for decorating tips on the Internet.*
- *If you're going to splurge, try looking for that one piece that will pull your room together. A nice leather club chair in the corner is a great piece to own, but a colorful throw rug will do more to make your room warm and livable.*
- *Mix and match. Don't be afraid to have that modern sofa next to an antique coffee table. When your rooms are a mixture of old and new, high-end and utilitarian, they're full of spirit and originality, just like the wonderful women I know in the South.*
- *Almost nothing scares off young suitors faster than a living room full of dolls and stuffed animals. Unless you're planning on living the single life forever, keep Fluffykins and Mrs. Snugglepuss safely tucked away in your closet.*

A true GRITS will love to help you decorate, whether you're redoing your five-bedroom house as a newly single mature woman or scraping together furniture to fill your tiny studio apartment. Nothing is more fun, or a cheaper way to transform a room, than pulling out all the furniture and inviting your girlfriends over for a painting party. Just be sure you get more of that paint on the walls than on each other!

GRITS GLOSSARY

Eclectic [e klek tik] **adj.** *1. In décor, a combination of different styles and periods. 2. A woman who wears a red shirt, orange pants, and green shoes. See also crazy, confident, and (just maybe) cool.*

PEARL OF WISDOM

Even the finest Chippendale chairs look awful when they're covered with cobwebs and dust. You may not be able to afford expensive antiques, but elbow grease is free. If your roommate or husband doesn't agree, try not to hold it against them. After all, you're getting a workout from all that dusting, mopping, and sweeping while they're just working the remote.

If you're ever in need, you know your GRITS friends will always be there to help you shop. A GRITS friend won't mind hitting every department store, yard sale, flea market, outlet mall, and consignment shop in town five times a week to find that perfect end table. She'll debate the merits of a simple print versus a big, floral pattern. She'll run her hands over carpet samples and swatches of paint. She'll help you choose your curtains, and she might even help you hang them. She'll look over dozens of prints with you before you decide that you'll just hang your old family photographs instead. Your husband or your boyfriend might moan and grumble, but a GRITS knows that you aren't wasting time; you're making a home. And remember, a day spent shopping with a friend is never a wasted day. That's my definition of heavenly.

From the time we're children, Southern women are taught not to brag about themselves. I agree that we shouldn't go around crowing about our own abilities; if we're truly good at something, our friends will do the bragging for us. Though we wouldn't dream of talking about ourselves, each of us has at least one special homemaking skill that we can be proud of. Think of your own home, and I'm sure there's something that you know you can be proud of: your good eye for arranging furniture, your skill with a needle, your famous cakes. Even if you're no domestic goddess, there's something that you can do better than all your friends, even if it's nothing more than finding the best bargains.

GRITS know that the best way to learn is from their friends. Organize a "skill swap" where you and your friends can exchange services. You can learn a new skill—some women are embarrassed to admit that even at the age of sixty, they can't sew a button—or you can just take advantage of what your friends know. You can share your own God-given talents. You can save some money in your homemaking. Best of all, though, you can spend a few hours sharing with your Southern girlfriends.

Everyone's skills are unique, but here are a few that you and your friends might share:

> *How to read music*
> *How to cook a favorite dish, or the basics of an ethnic cuisine*
> *How to trim split ends*
> *How to sew or knit*
> *How to scrapbook*
> *How to knit*
> *How to send and receive e-mail (It's harder than it seems for some of us!)*
> *How to save money on your taxes*
> *How to spend money on the best bargains in town*

Someone's in the Kitchen

We Southern girls love to cook up something with our friends, whether it's a batch of hot cayenne cheese sticks or a mess of trouble! Cooking saves money, saves our health, and maybe most important, eating a meal as a family around the table can bring everyone closer.

If you find it's too much trouble to cook up a meal from scratch every night, gather your girlfriends together and start a cooking club. Once a month, every member cooks one or two complete, freezable meals, and makes enough for every family in the group. The group then gets together and exchanges meals, packaged in disposable trays. Cooking a big batch isn't much more trouble than cooking one meal, and when you make the exchange, you have a variety of meals for several evenings. When you're exhausted from a day of work, shuttling the kids to soccer practice, and cleaning the floors, all you have to do is pull out a batch of Betty's famous chicken casserole and green beans amandine or Judy's three-bean chili and apple cobbler.

While it's true that you can learn cooking from a cooking class or a book, learning with a family member or a friend is easier and a lot more fun. A friend or a family member can show you just the right way to shake the cake batter to get the bubbles out, and she can teach you exactly how thick the gravy should be when you take it off the heat. A lot of cooking is about intuition and feel, and that's something that is best learned from a friend, not a stranger, and certainly not a book. A friend can teach you her family recipes, and you can share yours with her.

White Gloves and Sweet Tea: Entertaining and Manners

Southern women have always been gracious hostesses, and the reason should be obvious to anyone who knows us: We don't entertain out of duty; we entertain because we truly love people. We love to make a beautiful home, but it wouldn't be worth much if we didn't open our doors to friends and family. Southerners know the rules of etiquette, and we live by them. Now, I don't mean that we spread out twenty forks every time we set the table—though every Southern girl does like to set a table in the proper way—I mean that manners are important to us. To me, manners are about making people around you comfortable, about living graciously. We use manners with our friends because our friends are important to us, and we want to make them feel welcomed and proud to be our friends.

PEARL OF WISDOM

Sadly, some of our Instant GRITS don't have the training in manners that was once an important part of every Southern girl's education. Teach your daughters and granddaughters manners in a fun way by having a tea party in their honor. Each girl should dress in her finest dress, with white gloves, naturally, if she has them. At the beginning of the party, show the girls how to unfold a napkin, to dab their lips, to use a cup and a fork properly. Then, the girls can sit down to their own fancy little meal, and feel like the little ladies they undoubtedly are.

We Southerners love to throw a fancy affair, and I think we do it better than most anyone, but it's those wonderful, informal get-togethers with our friends that make life in the South so truly pleasant. Backyard cookouts, bonfires by the beach, card parties, picnics, or just a cup of coffee with the lady next door—we love any excuse to gather our friends and family together. From the time we're setting out the food to the hours of catching up after we've cleared the table, Southern entertaining is about being with our Southern friends and celebrating the flavor of the South.

A Blessing to Remember

My mother's meals were plentiful and made with the freshest meat and vegetables, with homemade cathead biscuits or cornbread, sometimes both, cooked in the old Southern style, with a pinch of this and just enough of that. Our small home was immaculate, and we kids were always warned to be on our best behavior. Mother's guests ran the gamut from next-door neighbors to the mayor of our small town.

One Saturday, my father invited both a business associate and the local pastor. Mother was in a tizzy because she didn't know the religious affiliation of the business associate, and she didn't want to make anyone uncomfortable. Mother decided that I would offer the blessing. Who could be uncomfortable around a cute eight-year-old with a long ponytail, a bright smile, and a gift of gab?

Unfortunately, she forgot to inform me. When everyone was gathered at the table and all heads bowed, Mother turned to me and asked me to offer the blessing. Being placed on the spot, in front of the preacher and his family and the stranger my dad had invited, I immediately forgot the blessing. I could remember "Now I lay me down to sleep," I could remember "God bless Mama, Daddy," but the dinner blessing was gone from my memory. I knew I had to say something, so I just plucked up my courage and said, "Dear Lord, thank you for this food. Now tuck back your ears and dive in!" Everyone thought it was pretty funny except Mother, who learned a valuable lesson in the finer art of entertaining that evening.

—Peggy DeLaughter
Alabama

A Silk Purse From a Pig's Ear

We Southern girls always like to help our friends and neighbors in times of trouble but, often, we're facing troubles of our own. When the company is downsizing, and money is tight, buying flowers or presents for our friends just isn't possible. Instead of going into debt, we should love the things that we have, especially our friends. Living life the Southern way means making do with what we have. Here are a few ways we can help each other without spending those precious pennies.

- Offer to walk dogs, baby-sit, or housesit. There is no gift more precious than time, and your overwhelmed friend will appreciate the opportunity to do a bit of living without worry.

- Do some research and find free things to do almost everywhere. Larger cities have free concerts, book readings, "nature" walks in the local park, and free museum days, and even smaller towns often have these events. Your local library and free weekly newspapers are a wonderful resource.

- When some of your friends are meeting at fancy restaurants, and the rest of you can barely afford a bucket of chicken, don't be jealous. You can make your own hoity-toity evening. Invite your best friend over and cook your favorite dishes together; don't splurge on anything fancy or expensive, just real, solid food. Pull out your candles, your linens, your best china, and sit down to a better meal than the miniscule portions of seared foie gras with kiwi sauce your friends are eating. Even chicken wings taste special when they're served on Grandma's china, and anything tastes better with a friend.

CHAPTER 10

Working Girls

"Always be smarter than the people who hire you."—LENA HORNE

"To those who have received honors, awards, and distinctions, I say well done. And to the C students, I say that you, too, may someday be president of the United States."—PRESIDENT GEORGE W. BUSH, TEXAS GRITS

The Southern women I grew up with could rise at dawn, work all day, and get home at night to whip up a dinner for their families. They could sew a warm quilt with nothing but a few old scraps. They could keep their families fed on less money than I spend on nail polish. They could do fine needlework and just as easily climb up a ladder to mend the roof. Why, they could even step behind the plow if the men were short a hand.

These days, my manicure and I are thankful that most women aren't driving a team of mules, but we're still getting our hands dirty bringing home the grits and boiling them up in a pan. Southern women today work just as hard making warm and wonderful homes for their families. Whether they work in a high-rise, a factory, or a restaurant, volunteer at the hospital or at home, or take care of the people they love better than anyone else in the world, Southern women are not strangers to hard work.

Work wouldn't be the same without our Southern friends by our side. We meet some of our best friends on the job. They teach us the ropes, and support us when we get rope burn. Friends help us find a job, and then make it bearable to show up every morning. When we work from home like I do—or work making a home for our families—friends keep us connected to the world, and they teach us the very best way to clean our silver without poisoning the tuna casserole.

Add a Pearl, Drop a Pearl

- *In these times, when the nine-to-five job has become the five-to-nine job for many of us, work has become the best place to cultivate friendships. Just try to keep personal affairs out of business. I don't need to tell a Southern girl that a loud discussion of the men you flirted with last night is as inappropriate in the boardroom as a discussion of your company's latest legal problems is at your niece's bridal shower.*
- *It's best to avoid office romance, but sometimes Mr. Right just happens to be sitting in the next cubicle. Keep any extracurricular activities, from your first furtive kiss to your furniture-flinging breakup, between the two of you. There's a time and place for everything.*
- *Make sure that any favor you ask of a friend at work is something that you would comfortably do yourself. Being a true friend means that you don't compromise your friend's job or sanity.*
- *While the office grapevine is often the most fun you'll have all year, there's a big difference between spreading the news and spreading gossip. Gossip at work can harm, and no GRITS worth her pearls would ever use gossip to bring another woman down. We've got to stick together, darling, not tear each other apart.*
- *Remember, just because your friends don't go into an office doesn't mean that they don't work. Work-at-home mothers or*

174 | Working Girls

full-time homemakers have responsibilities, too, so don't impose
on them by asking too many favors or, even worse, act like
you're the only one working around here.

Cramming and Jamming

GRITS don't begin work when they interview for their first job. From the time they're little girls learning to make biscuits by their mothers' sides to the time they're teaching their grandchildren table manners, GRITS work as hard as, if not harder than, any man. Not that I'm complaining. I'm just pointing out that, no matter how hard you try, no man will ever understand how hard you work as well as another woman. Believe me, I've tried four times, and they all thought they were helping with the housework when they picked up their dirty underwear once a week.

When we're schoolgirls, or even taking orders at our first job at the local burger joint, most GRITS come home to their families each night. College or marriage is the first time most Southern girls work on their own, and don't have Mama and Daddy by their sides to spur them on. For many Southern women, college is the first time our girlfriends, rather than our families, help us get through the working day.

Though it might come as a surprise to some parents, we GRITS actually spend some of our time at college studying. We naturally try to take the same classes as our girlfriends, not to cheat (a real Pearl Girl doesn't need or want to cheat), pass notes, or even whine about difficult professors. We take the same classes because even studying becomes bearable when you do it with your favorite girls!

WELL, I DECLARE

The effort we Southern girls put into studying is not a new thing; we Southerners have long believed in the importance of education. Back in 1836, the Texas Declaration of Independence stated: "It is an axiom in political science that unless a people are educated and enlightened, it is idle to expect the continuance of civil liberty or the capacity for self-government." In other words, you really need to take the time to learn more than the candidates' names before you vote.

Southern girls aren't all good looks and charming smiles, though all the ladies I know have both. We know that to make it as the doctors, teachers, saleswomen, writers, and mothers that we'll become, we'll need knowledge. People outside of the South sometimes don't give us credit for having brains as well as beauty—our natural good manners keep us from bragging about ourselves—but those who are smart wouldn't want to argue against a Southern lady lawyer, negotiate against a GRITS businesswoman or, even worse, try to sneak something past a GRITS mother. The fact is, we Southern ladies don't just primp our hair and pluck our eyebrows; we also work to make sure that our brains are in good shape. We work hard, and we expect our college girlfriends to work hard, too, whether they're fifteen-year-old brainiacs jumping ahead three grades or eighty-year-old grandmothers finally going back to get that high school diploma. After all, we need our study partners to be on their toes, and we're looking forward to the day when we sit on the Board of Directors or team teach with our girlfriends at our sides.

PEARL OF WISDOM

Not so long ago, women in colleges lived in all-female dorms, and visits from men were strictly limited; many Southern parents wish things were still that way. If you're having trouble convincing your daughter to live in a single-sex dorm, remind her what she looks like walking to the shower at seven in the morning. Better yet, take a picture: It's worth a thousand nags.

The best part of studying is quitting time, of course. We Southern girls might work hard, but we aren't married to those books, for goodness' sake. If you think that one Southern girl is fun, imagine a dorm or sorority house with a hundred of us! When the books are down, the party is on. When you have a group of giggling Southern gals, hanging out in the dorm can be almost as fun as painting the town.

WELL, I DECLARE

We've all heard the myth that the average college freshman packs on fifteen pounds in the first year of school. Is it true? Well, a Cornell University professor has recently found that the average college freshman gains about four pounds during the first twelve weeks of school. Whew, honey, watch that pizza and beer, and make sure you pack on fifteen girlfriends instead!

Rat Year

In 1968, I went to college and began learning the ropes of being a freshman (or a "rat," as we were known back then). I remember fresh-

man "rat races," a "Miss Charming" pageant, communal bathrooms, being friends with a girl named Jimmy, cooking up fine cuisine on a popcorn popper, and wearing raincoats over slacks on Sunday because it was the rule. Most of all, it was a time to live and grow with other young women, and to create memories with them. If I had known everything that would happen, I might have been too scared to pursue my dreams. That's why I often remind myself of Eleanor Roosevelt's famous quotation: "Do one thing every day that scares you." My time at college was the start of that great adventure.

—Mitzi Groom
Kentucky

WELL, I DECLARE

Worried that your little girl will drink irresponsibly once she goes off to school? A national survey found that the majority of college students drink two or fewer drinks a week. Sounds like a lot of GRITS have been listening to their mamas!

Reasons Your College Friends Are Special

- They don't see anything strange about dieting all day, then sharing a well-earned pizza at two in the morning.

- *They share your belief that toilet paper and shaving cream are important assets in the war between the sexes.*
- *At least one of them knows enough calculus and organic chemistry to help the rest of you pass.*
- *They teach you the joys of car trips. To this day, I know there's no better vacation than five girls in a ratty old Buick heading off to do damage in Myrtle Beach, Daytona Beach, or Corpus Christi.*
- *When you're flush, they'll help you spend your money on a night on the town, but when Daddy won't send any more, they'd just as soon spend a night watching bad movies on television and gossiping about the boys in Kappa Alpha.*
- *They teach you what's in a Kamikaze, a Stinger, a Flaming Dr Pepper, and a Tequila Sunrise. And they make sure you get home safely when you've had them all at once.*
- *They've seen you without your "face" on, and they didn't laugh or pity you.*
- *You've seen them without their "face" on, so you never have to worry that they're too perfect to be friends with you.*

If we can't hang out in our dorms, we love to go out with our Southern girlfriends. Whether we're a Georgia Tech student going to the Varsity in Atlanta for a chili dog or a UGA student listening to our favorite band at the 40 Watt in Athens, a Southern girl knows how to live it up in her college town.

We've got spirit, yes we do, we've got spirit, how 'bout you? If you're a GRITS, the answer is easy; you've got enough spirit to fill up a room—even a room of Massachusetts sourpusses. Every school in the South has some cheer or chant. Here's a quick guide to just a handful.

University of Alabama

Cheer: Roll Tide

Pros: *A couple of simple and cheap household products—a roll of toilet paper and some laundry detergent to be precise—can serve as an impromptu cheering device. Bama girls are fit to be Tide!*

Cons: *It's hard to look fashionable when you're walking around with toilet paper on a stick.*

University of Georgia

Cheer: Sic 'Em, Woof, Woof, Woof

Pros: *There's nothing like a stadium full of students barking to raise the roof.*

Cons: *Being ladylike and barking like a dog don't really go together.*

Ole Miss

Cheer: Hotty Toddy

Pros: *Catchy fight song with a long tradition.*

Cons: *Sounds a bit like you're ordering a glass of liquor or a male stripper.*

Arkansas Razorbacks

Cheer: Woo Pig Sooey

Pros: *Volume. A couple of thousand kids shouting "sooey" can rock any stadium.*

Cons: *Sometimes livestock will answer the call. Sometimes the men who answer are even worse.*

Georgia Tech

Cheer: *Ramblin' Wreck*

Pros: *Catchy music and an excuse to bring out some old cars.*

Cons: *Nothing is nerdier than a fight song that talks with pride about being an engineer.*

University of Tennessee

Cheer: *Fight, Vols, Fight*

Pros: *Your opponents scratch their heads and wonder, "What on earth's a vol?"*

Cons: *What on earth's a vol? (That's a Tennessee volunteer, for you Yankees.)*

University of Florida

Cheer: *"The Gator Chomp": The band plays the music from Jaws while the students clamp their arms opened and closed, imitating an alligator.*

Pros: *A good workout for that flab under the arms.*

Cons: *Umm, they're the Gators. Wasn't that Jaws movie about a shark?*

Austin Peay

Cheer: *Let's Go Peay!*

Pros: *The cheer certainly makes this East Tennessee school stand out.*

Cons: *I can't think of one Southern girl who wants to shout about her bodily functions in public.*

Whether she's a college graduate or entering the work world without even a high school degree, every Southern woman needs a hand to help her up. In every working woman's life, there is some special woman who guides her through the rough patches: a mother, a boss, a co-worker, or just a friend. This woman teaches her never to ask a favor of her boss on a Monday morning, how to get decent projects thrown her way, and just what "business casual" means. She has experience, and she's a good enough friend to share it with a woman who's just coming up.

There are lots of people who call this special guide in a working woman's life a mentor; I prefer just to call her a friend. She's the older sister whose advice you seek on matters as small as whether your skirt is too short and as large as whether to take a transfer to a new city. She's willing to talk even when she's wading through a dozen of her own projects. She's been where you're standing, and like any good Southern girl, she's willing to lend a hand to a friend.

PEARL OF WISDOM

Special friends who serve as mentors don't exist just in the workplace. At places of worship throughout the South, women serve as "spiritual mentors" to help women new to their faiths. The experience and wisdom that they've gained through years of worship help those who are just starting to grow spiritually.

Someday, if you succeed (and of course you will; you're a GRITS), you'll see some other young woman straight out of school, dressed in a brand-new suit, and looking for the coffee machine. For goodness' sake, tell her to avoid that awful coffee like the plague, and lend her a helping hand with her career.

Getting By, and Getting Even

We Southern women look like angels and work like the devil. Some days, it feels like making five hundred copies, cleaning up the grape juice from your new white rug, or serving yet another refill on table five is just about the last thing you can bear. Face it: as good as we are at whatever we set our minds to do, there are days when we'd just as soon anyone else do it.

The Homecoming

World War II was hard on women left behind while their husbands and sons went to fight the war. With nothing but a tiny military paycheck, the women left behind had to scrape to make ends meet. Mother went to work for Goodyear Mills in Cartersville, Georgia. For working a twelve-hour-a-day shift, she received eight dollars a week. After putting a roof over her family's heads and food on the table, there wasn't money left over for store-bought clothing. After mother put in a full day at the mill, she and my grandmother sewed all their dresses, shirts, and pants.

My father was one of the brave soldiers who made it home. He had been gone for five years, alienated from familiar surroundings, and my mother didn't even recognize him when he came off the war train at Kingston, Georgia's depot.

Several years went by, and the South's pockets began to bulge a little. After doing without for so many years, my mother and sisters decided that they had earned an all-day shopping spree. My father, still vulnerable from the stress of the war, was persuaded to drive all the girls over to Rome, Georgia.

He parked the car in front of Murphy's Department Store, and the girls rushed in, looking at every item on the shelves and the racks. Father skulked outside, smoking one cigarette after another, pacing, trying not to get aggravated with Mother. After several hours of waiting, he entered the store and said gently, "Rosa, let's go." It was as if he were addressing a brood of deaf mares.

The ladies ignored my father, and continued to waltz down aisle after aisle. Then my mother stopped in her tracks and stared right across the store. "Look at that woman across the store, the one looking at me, she looks just like me!"

Father nearly lost his breath laughing, and the aunts started roaring. My poor mother had no idea why they were laughing. Finally, her sister spoke up: "Rosa, that's a store-length mirror you're looking into."

In all those years of making do, I guess Mother had forgotten what it was like inside a shopping store. At least after all his years of deprivation, Father got one good laugh, and the family got a story they could chuckle about for years to come.

—Cora Sue Glass
Georgia

Those difficult days are the best time to remember what's so special about you. You might have two reports and a presentation due, you might be working double shifts, your children might be holy terrors but, honey, it'll all be fine in the end because you've got your Southern mothers behind you, and your Southern sisters by your side. You're a GRITS, you're special and, honey, you not only get by, you get by in style.

Five Ways to Get Through the Day

- *Talk to your friends. Sure, it wastes a few minutes, but let the boss lose his temper if he wants. Getting it all out lets you get on with it.*
- *Remember who you're working for. Whether it means taking out a picture of your children or husband, or just looking in the mirror for a couple of minutes, remember that you're not working for your boss, but for the ones you love.*
- *Close your eyes, and take in a long, slow, deep breath through your nose. Slowly exhale through your mouth. Repeat ten times. You'll feel better, and you won't have to pay Rainbow down at the yoga studio fifty dollars to teach you how to breathe.*
- *Throw a hissy fit. Just remember to do it by yourself, or with your closest girlfriend, with the door to your office, or the door to a bathroom stall, closed tightly. Ladies don't throw hissy fits in public.*
- *Take a minute and think of your great-grandmother raising up a dozen children, washing clothes in the creek, and giving a helping hand out in the field. No matter how hard your life seems now, it's easy compared to hers, and it was her hard work that helped you get where you are.*

In the end, getting by means being yourself. You may find yourself wearing your fingers to the bone earning a few extra dollars for your millionaire boss. You may be cleaning up for a husband and children who don't take the time to thank you. You may be screwing the same bolt into the same piece of machinery on the assembly line day after day. No matter what, hold your head high and think of all the other women out there who are doing their best to make this country work.

Lunchtime Round Table

All too often, lunchtime conversation centers around your boss's endless demands or what happened on reality television last night. While it's great to blow off some steam just having fun, it's also wonderful to know more about your co-workers than what they eat on their sandwiches and how they decorate their cubicles. These are some lunchtime topics that can generate meaningful conversation. You might feel a little awkward or hokey posing these questions at first, but most co-workers will willingly play along. When your friendships start to deepen, you'll be glad you went out on a limb.

- A distant relative has died, leaving you with a million dollars. The only string attached is that you must spend the entire amount within one month. What do you do?
- What's the most romantic thing you've ever done? What's the most romantic thing you'd like to do?
- The president wants to take a well-earned vacation, so he leaves you in charge for a week while he jets off to a distant Pacific island. What's your first order of business?

- *If you had to be locked in an elevator with a celebrity for twenty-four hours, who would you choose and why?*
- *If money were no object, would you rather spend a month living it up in the capitals of Europe, relaxing on a deserted tropical island, or exploring the deepest Amazon?*

For me, holding my head high has meant taking the time to pull myself together, even when I was juggling business deals, cranky relatives, and putting the finishing touches on a chapter. Sure, I could have thrown on some sweatpants and thrown my hair into a ponytail, but we Southern women know that feeling ready for anything translates into feeling strong and feeling confident. Now, I'm not saying that all women should be this way; sugar, if you feel best dressed in a housedress and curlers, more power to you. The point is, being comfortable and feeling your best helps you get through those rough days.

PEARL OF WISDOM

I know it's the style among a certain crowd these days, but I'm sorry: no self-respecting woman should wear pajamas in public.

If you find you can't get by, you can always get even. Southern ladies don't spend their time plotting revenge; we try to smooth things over and get on as best we can. Still, I think we all laughed when we saw Dolly Parton dream of lassoing her lecherous boss in *9 to 5*. She behaved like a lady on the outside, but inside, she was dreaming of having that no-good man hog-tied.

Unless you work in the rodeo, I wouldn't recommend roping and hog-tying anyone at work. You can, however, get your revenge the way that we Southern girls always have: by being the best GRITS that we can. We treat our enemies with smiles; we go forward looking and feeling good. If you can outclass them, outsmile them, outwork them, and outblonde them, you'll win everyone, sometimes even your enemy, over to your side. Even if those enemies are the kind that will still stab us in the back, we just turn away; Southern women would rather not dirty our pretty little hands slinging mud. The best part of taking the high road is that we come off looking like GRITS. The best revenge is being successful, and any Pearl Girl who stays true to herself is a success in my book.

PEARL OF WISDOM

My mother said: "If you can't say anything nice, don't say anything at all." Honey, that advice doesn't just apply to the playground. As fun as office, or neighborhood, gossip is, keep those dirty little secrets where they belong, in private. Remember, as soon as you start slinging mud, you start losing ground!

With a Little Help From My Friends

Oftentimes, successful women in movies or television are hard, lonely, and bitter. I say, those movies must have been written by men! Successful women have never done it alone. Whether it was their mothers, their daughters, or their best friends, women who made it to the top had someone giving them a lift up.

WELL, I DECLARE

A recent study found that eighty-two percent of female executives were involved in organized sports after elementary school, versus sixty-one percent of women in the general population. Maybe it's their competitive spirit that got them ahead, or maybe it was learning to play well with others. Whatever the reason, get out those track shoes, pom-poms, and gym shorts, girls, and I'll meet you in the boardroom!

I've always thought that we Southerners define "success" differently than people in other parts of the country. You can have the diamonds, the Mercedes Benz, the big house, a fancy title and, goodness knows, many of us do, but if you don't have friends and family, you can't truly call yourself a success. There are Southern women who work on assembly lines, who make burgers, who check you out at the store, and they'll never have a mansion or even a dental plan, but if they have a group of wonderful GRITS to share their lives with, they're successful. In my mind, the homemaker who's barely making ends meet, but giving her children hot meals and warm hugs, is more of a success than the woman who neglects her family while she goes off to run the world. We Southerners find our success not just in the bank vault, but in the vaults of our hearts. Maybe it's because our region was so poor for so long, but I think that we Southern girls know that true wealth isn't something that you can put on your charge card.

GRITS GLOSSARY

Network [net wərk] v. *A fancy name for what we Southern girls have always done: talked 'til we're blue in the face.* Networking means building up connections and then using them to further your career (and if you're Southern, furthering the careers of your friends).

PEARL OF WISDOM

"Don't confuse fame with success. Madonna is one; Helen Keller is the other."—Erma Bombeck

You Go, Girl!: Southern Women Who've Made Their Mark

We Southern girls love to see our Southern sisters who have made it. Here are just a few of the many Southern women who have lifted up their lives with their Southern girlfriends by their sides.

Condoleezza Rice: Dr. Condoleezza Rice hails from Birmingham, Alabama. In spite of being born into the time of segregation in the South, she worked her way up through the world of academics, becoming a professor of political science and provost of prestigious Stanford University. She became National Security Advisor in President George W. Bush's first administration, and in his second administration she is the first woman, white or black, to hold the office of Secretary of State.

Dr. Rice is not some stiff, boring woman hiding in an ivory tower. She finds strength in religion and enjoys the

South's other religion: football. She's known for being charming and gracious. This lovely lady is known as "Condi" to her friends. She gets a great deal of her strength from her parents. When she was a little girl, her family visited the White House, and she looked at the building and said that although her color kept her out, someday, she'd be in that house. I'm proud to say that this GRITS was right!

Naomi and Wynonna Judd: Naomi is a small-town girl from Ashland, Kentucky, who gave birth to daughter Wynonna while she was still in high school. Naomi divorced when her children were little, and she worked hard to make ends meet.

Naomi and Wynonna moved to Nashville to pursue their country music dreams, but it was a bit of chance that landed them a break. Naomi, a nurse, treated a record producer's child after a car accident. The producer was impressed enough with Naomi to give her a recording deal. The Judds' first album was a hit, and they won the first of their five Grammy awards.

Naomi was diagnosed with a serious liver disease in 1990, and the Judds gave their farewell tour to thank the fans the following year. Naomi survived with the help of her family and her faith, and she has since written an autobiography and two children's books. Wynonna went on to a very successful solo career. And as if there weren't enough wonderful women in this family, daughter Ashley is a Hollywood star!

The Judd ladies are an inspiration to Southern women. They started with nothing but their hopes and became a family of superstars. As Wynonna says: "Mom and I . . . felt like the poster children for all the dreamers. We were two girls from Ashland who weren't afraid to try." These ladies sang like the angels and fought like the devil, but they loved each other through struggle, triumph, and tragedy.

The Jarvis Family: Ann Maria Reeves Jarvis was a West Virginia woman who spent her life bringing peace to her world. She organized Mothers Day Work Clubs to raise money for medicine and to improve the poor health and sanitary conditions that led to tuberculosis. Ann was a deeply religious woman, and her goal was to spread God's love to all people, no matter what color uniform they might wear. During the Civil War, she fought for the clubs to remain neutral and serve the men fighting and dying on both sides. In 1865, she organized a Mothers Friendship Day to bring together soldiers and neighbors from the Union and the Confederacy, and the event became so successful that it continued for years after the war.

After her mother's death, daughter Anna spent years lobbying for a national Mother's Day, and eventually President Woodrow Wilson set aside the second Sunday in May for the celebration. These days, a lot of people will tell you that Mother's Day was invented by the card companies, but the truth is that it was the work of a devoted daughter who wanted to honor her mother's work.

A Silk Purse From a Pig's Ear

As hard as Southern girls work, as wonderful as all the women I know are, even they sometimes spend a couple of months, or even a couple of years, unsuccessfully looking for work. Even worse, after we've had personal and financial successes, we may find ourselves do-

ing work we're overqualified for; business executives find themselves
working in boutiques, lawyers find themselves serving coffee. We try
to put our best face on for the world, but it's hard to smile sometimes
when the unemployment checks are running out and there are three
hundred applications for each good job.

- *Remember: Every job is worth doing, and worth doing well.
  Take pride in your work, whether you're sitting behind the big
  desk or emptying the trash cans. You can bring something
  special to every job, and you can learn something from every
  job, so do your best. If your friend is at a new job, take the
  time to tell her how proud you are of what she's doing.*
- *Sometimes, knowing that other women are in the same situation
  as you can make you feel better. Talk to your friends who are
  unemployed or, if they're all lucky enough to have work, look
  for support groups. The Internet is a great resource for finding
  groups of people in the same boat as you.*
- *Many women are looking for work after years staying home
  with children, or years on the same job. Looking for work
  when you're in your fifties or sixties can be a challenge. In
  your résumé and in interviews, don't highlight your age, but
  do highlight your years of real-life experience.*
- *Don't be afraid to ask for help from your friends. Have at least
  two sets of eyes look at each résumé and each interview outfit,
  and you can go out with the confidence that your friends have
  missed nothing.*
- *Not every job involves going into an office. I have operated my
  own businesses in apparel and, obviously, writing. Look at
  your own God-given talents, and see what you can offer to
  others. You may need to take a few courses, but with a little
  hard work, you can operate your own tailoring, accounting,*

baby-sitting, cleaning, writing, baking, or computer business. We Southern women are modest, so we often overlook those things that we do well; brainstorm with your friends about what you do best. Don't waste your talents; invest them in the world, and they'll come back to you tenfold!

A Friend for Every Season

"I find friendship to be like wine, raw when new, ripened with age, the true old man's milk and restorative cordial."—THOMAS JEFFERSON, VIRGINIA GRITS

CHAPTER II

We've Got Trouble

"The strength of the pack is the wolf, and the strength of the wolf is the pack."—RUDYARD KIPLING

"If you don't like something, change it. If you can't change it, change your attitude. Don't complain."
—MAYA ANGELOU, MISSOURI

Girls raised in the South know that if one thing is certain in this life, it's change. One minute you're a little girl chasing junebugs out back of the house, and the next you're chasing after a crazy toddler of your own. Turn your head, and your little girl is walking down the aisle. Before you know it, you'll be spoiling the grandchildren, and the great-grandchildren come right on their heels.

Even our beloved South is constantly changing: Highways and cable television have opened up our sleepy little backwater towns, big businesses have brought jobs—and a whole lot of different accents—to our cities, and we've gone from raising cotton and peanuts to raising capital and campaign donations. Our grandparents might not recognize much about the South we live in, but they would recognize those things that have remained constant: our values, heritage, and the importance we place on family and friends. Through all the changes, and all the troubles they bring, we've stayed strong because we've held on to what we believe in.

Throughout our lifetimes, the roles friends play in our lives change, but the importance of those friends stays the same. Those friends see us through the hard times. We Southern girls continue to make friends throughout our lives, and we also work hard to make sure that those old friendships last throughout life's changes.

Keeping It Together When Things Fall Apart

- *When a friend moves away, she'll miss her favorite GRITS from home, especially if she's stuck someplace where home fries are on the menu rather than good old hominy. Regular cards, letters, and phone calls will lift her spirits or, better yet, remind her of why she needs to come back home to her friends. She'll especially appreciate it if you grab the video camera and get all her friends to leave her a personal message. When your friend is feeling lonely, she can pop the tape in her VCR and remember all the wonderful friends who love and miss her.*

- *When your daughter is joining the Hare Krishnas, your ex-husband is marrying a twenty-five-year-old, and your dream home turns out to be built on a landfill, life can get a wee bit stressful. Minding your body can help keep your mind clear and happy. To keep yourself strong and healthy during a life change, enlist a friend to help you safeguard your health. Shop for healthy foods—rather than junk that will just make you feel worse in the end—and take time out to cook and eat those foods with a friend. Schedule time together each week or, better yet, each day, to walk, jog, or do your favorite exercise together. Listen to your friend when she nags you, and don't let her off easily, either. Maintaining healthy habits is difficult at any time, but especially when you're under stress, and a friend can help you stay the course when nothing else in your life seems to be on track.*

- *Southern girls don't move on from their friends just because they're moving on with their lives. When you're immersed in a new job, a new home, or a new relationship, it's easy to forget the girls who've stood by you through the years. Take some time to let your old girlfriends know that they still matter in your life; send them a card or a gift or, better yet, reserve an evening just for your oldest friends, no matter how long it's been since you saw them last. The new men and women you meet are wonderful, but it's the people who knew you when you were nothing who are the most precious treasures in your heart.*

- *When a friend falls ill, take the time to give her more than a perfunctory visit to the hospital, and let her know that, no matter what, you'll be there by her side. Serious illness such as cancer can rob us not only of our health, but of our image of ourselves as attractive, feminine women. If a friend is undergoing chemotherapy, for instance, take her to shop for wigs or attractive hats and scarves before she actually begins to lose her hair. Make a day out of finding a look that is attractive on her, and take the time to tell her how lovely she is. Some women find it easier to shave their heads before the hair begins to fall out rather than face finding clumps in the shower morning after morning, so if your friend is sporting the new wig even before treatment begins, support her decision. Once she is undergoing therapy, remember that many cancer treatments may leave her feeling weak and sick, and she may be in no mood for cheering up. Sometimes the best role you may play is just sitting quietly by her side.*

Southern mothers teach their daughters to hold their heads high, to walk through life with poise and grace, whether they're members sipping tea at the country club or employees washing the glasses. When people see GRITS, they think that they could stand through anything on their own; a Southern girl is always calm and composed, whether she's competing in an important race or a tornado has just made off with her roof.

PEARL OF WISDOM

"Trouble is part of your life, and if you don't share it, you don't give the person who loves you a chance to love you enough."
—Dinah Shore, Tennessee

Southern girlfriends know better. Our friends may put on a brave face for the world, but we know that, inside, their hearts are racing a mile a minute. No matter how much their friends are smiling under pressure, GRITS know that they can use a hand to hold and a shoulder to cry on. When life brings the troubles and pressure, it's sure nice to have a Southern girl by your side.

Music Festival

The piano and I were not the best of friends. My parents, bless their hearts, wanted their daughters to be "well rounded," so as soon as I entered the second grade, my mother called Mrs. Norton over on Magnolia Street so that I could begin my piano lessons. My sister Priscilla was an excellent piano student, so my parents were expecting the same from me, but we sisters couldn't have been more different. I couldn't even play the scales without looking at my fingers. I was supposed to practice each piece ten times and record my progress with a tally mark. I must confess that I did let that pencil get away from me sometimes (some might say I cheated). Needless to say, my progress wasn't quite up there with Priscilla's.

Even though I wasn't proving a little prodigy, my parents encouraged me to enter the Florence Music Festival, sponsored by the Florence Music Club. Well, I was not at all pleased by the prospect, especially when I learned that Mrs. McWright from the junior high would be one of the judges. I suppose she was just a strict teacher, but from my second-grade perspective, it was like being asked to play music in front of a drill sergeant. Just when it was starting to sound unbearable, though, I learned that my best friend, Mary Wills Hatfield, was also playing. I decided that, with her at my side, I could do it.

Mrs. Norton and I selected "March of the Wooden Soldiers." I liked the way that my left hand crossed over my right to hit the high C at the end. For once, I practiced that song upside-down and backward until I could hear and see myself playing it in my sleep.

Mary Wills went before me, and she seemed to do just fine. With my best friend making it through the ordeal, I knew that I could, too. They called my name and I sat down. I played the piece without a blip until that final high C at the end. I heard the note in my head, but

I just didn't play it. I walked proudly to the door, but before I touched the knob, I realized that I had forgotten the last note. I turned on my heels and ran like I was being thrown out at first base, slid onto the piano bench, and played that last note. Plunk! I can still hear it to this day.

With every person in the audience laughing, I walked proudly to the door. It wasn't until I reached the room where the other children were waiting that I began to cry. Boy, was I glad Mary Wills was there at that moment! She didn't even laugh at me; she just said how great I had been.

I guess the judges weren't the ogres I thought they were, because even with the timing of that last high C I earned a "Superior." In my case, practice sure didn't make perfect, but having my best friend along did make things easier. Though I didn't find it funny at the time, at least we all have something to laugh at, and I'm sure everyone is as glad as I am that I don't ever have to play a piano again!

—Henrietta Hardy
Alabama

Living together means facing troubles together. The South I grew up in was a land of farms—and for many Southerners, it still is. Southerners learned that when the drought or the boll weevils came, everyone suffered. The only way to survive was to give and receive help from our Southern neighbors. What little we had was spread around, and if we weren't rich, at least we still had each other. When problems come up today, it's much the same. When a hurricane hits, it doesn't just hit your house; it hits all of your friends and neighbors. Recession, terrorism, and crime affect all of us. When we face trouble, Southern girls stand strong together.

Recently, my good friend Sandy Eichelberger stopped by my house, and tears were running down her face. Although I've known her for fifteen years, I've seen her in tears only once or twice, so I knew something dreadful must have happened. She confessed the truth to me: She had attempted to straighten and dye her hair without professional help. To some women, her disaster may not seem that awful, but many Southern girls will understand that losing your looks is one of the worst things in life. When Sandy had arrived, I was surprised to see that she was wearing a beautiful wig that made her look like Shania Twain (in fact, we later started calling her "Shania"). But when she pulled that beautiful wig off, she was nearly bald, and what little hair that was left was in no condition to be seen in public. I felt so bad for her that I had to cry right along. "I can't believe that this happened to me. I'm in denial," Sandy cried. We both thought a minute about Shania and her new look, and then yelled simultaneously, "Shania!" We started laughing hysterically through our tears. Maybe you had to be there, but it was two friends laughing together to get through the hard times. We were just a couple of Southern girls getting through a disaster the best way we could: laughing and crying with each other.

WELL, I DECLARE

"Recession is when a neighbor loses his job. Depression is when you lose yours."—*President Ronald Reagan*

My sister Becky is not just my sister, but also my best friend; in fact, we're so close that we share the same driveway! A few years ago, Becky's daughter was spending the night with a friend, but she called late at night, homesick, and asked for us to come get her. It was an hour away, and Becky did not want to go alone, so she called me to come with her. Normally, when we go out, we have to take a big old van, since Becky has five children and I have three, but this night, with just the three of us, we got to take my husband's truck, and not some huge "mommy mobile." We listened to loud music, chatted, and smoked—it was like a "housewives gone bad" night on the town.

We picked up Becky's daughter without incident, but about halfway home, Becky said, "Our gas situation doesn't look so good." Out in backwoods Alabama in the middle of the night, though, we had to try to make it. We almost did, but about four miles from home, we sputtered to a stop on a dark, curvy road. We had only passed a few houses, and were at least a mile from the nearest pay phone. We thought we were in trouble, but we didn't expect shooting to start! But then, from behind some bushes, someone started firing.

Being two people in a crisis—and sisters at that—we of course started to argue. Should we run from the truck and risk the fire? Being the eldest, Becky won. Before I even knew what was happening, she was running through the night for a pay phone, and I was soothing her daughter, now very much awake and very scared.

At that moment, a face appeared at the window. He had hardly any teeth, his hair was long and unkempt, and his beard almost reached his belt. I was screaming at the top of my lungs, but if I had stopped for a minute, I would have seen his kind eyes. He brought his daughter over from his truck, and told me the shooter was nuts (pretty *obvious). He told me his daughter lived in the red, white, and blue house around the curve and could help us. I looked at Grizzly Adams and swallowed hard, wondering whether I could trust him. With the gunfire coming closer, though, I took a leap of faith. Sure enough, she did live in a red, white, and blue house, just around the corner. They not only let me use their phone, they went out in their car to rescue Becky from the unsafe road. Were we glad when Becky's husband drove up to take us home!*

I saw that kind man several years later at the grocery store. He still lives in the same house, and he may still be helping people escape his crazy neighbor. Becky and I learned some lessons that night: Make sure you have plenty of gas and, more important, you sure can't judge a book by its cover.

—Renee McMinn-Smith
Alabama

Ramblin' Girl

Hank Williams, Sr. sang that the Lord made him a ramblin' man, but he could have just as easily been talking about a Southern girl. There was a time when several generations of Southerners would live under one roof, and we might sleep in the same room from the time we were toddlers to the time we were grandmothers. While some Southern families still do stay rooted in the same homes for generations, most of us are going to move at least once in our lives. For many military families in particular, moving is a way of life. "Army brats" may easily attend school in California one year, and travel to Germany the next.

WELL, I DECLARE

According to the U.S. Census Bureau, the average American moves about twelve times in her lifetime, and about one in six Americans moves each year. Don't worry, though, that one of your six closest girlfriends is liable to pack up and move to Detroit this year; in most cases, movers stayed within their own county.

Whether we're college girls away from home for the first time or moving into the nursing home, moving is one of the most difficult changes we can make. We're leaving the familiar streets, our familiar yard and, most importantly, our familiar friends. We find ourselves alone in a new city, and suddenly there's no shoulder to cry on when the movers break our grandmother's best china. We can ease the transition for our friends who move by staying in touch, by letting them know that, just because they've moved from our blocks, they haven't moved from our hearts. Nothing can make moving easy, especially for us Southern girls for whom home is everything, but the comforting voices of old friends can sure ease the way.

PEARL OF WISDOM

Friends don't let friends pack alone. Whether she's moving across the street or across the country, helping your friend to pack her possessions securely is a wonderful, generous gift. And don't forget to "accidentally" slip some pictures of her old friends into her boxes. That way, when she's overwhelmed with moving into her new home, memories of the loved and the familiar can give her some comfort when she least expects it.

Moving isn't just about leaving old friends; it's about making new ones. On the day we move into a bare house, with walls that have no pictures and no memories for us, we might feel like the most lonely people in the world. A wave from a friendly neighbor can make those lonely first days feel a little less empty. An invitation to a backyard cookout, or a plate of homemade cookies, helps us feel that maybe this strange new place can be home after all. When new neighbors move in, take the time to ring their doorbells and say hello. It's what you'd want in their place, and it's the Southern way.

Guardian Angels

My husband, Wesley, and I met in college in Oklahoma in 1950. Two weeks before his time in the Marine Reserves was scheduled to end, the Korean War broke out. He joined the Oklahoma National Guard's 45th Infantry Division, and he was scheduled to train for several months in Louisiana before shipping out to Korea. He asked me to marry him before he left with his division. On his three-day Christmas leave, we were married. At the time, women could marry at eighteen, but men under twenty-one needed parental consent. My husband was only nineteen, so he had to call his mother to come across town and sign our marriage license for us!

I was a brand-new military wife on my way to a strange town. We had no car, so we rented a house sight unseen at Rosepine, about twenty miles from Camp Polk, Louisiana. The bus dropped us off on a slow stretch of highway at about nine o'clock on a Sunday night. We were stuck in the middle of nowhere without our luggage—which we'd have to pick up at the bus depot—and without a clue as to what to do. With no other good options, we started walking.

Thankfully, a couple of guardian angels stopped their car on the way home from church and asked us where we were going. When we told them, the husband and wife gave each other a meaningful glance, then told us to hop in. Our "house," as the landlord called it, turned out to be six miles from the highway on a dirt road. It was nothing more than a small, rough log cabin. The "rooms" were nothing more than four sections divided up by old blankets slung over clotheslines. The husband offered to take my husband to Camp Polk, since he was due in before midnight, and they insisted that we not spend another minute in that house. They welcomed us into their own home until we could find another place. Without them, I don't know how we would have made it through the night, much less our first weeks, in that strange town.

About two days later, they found us a room in a home in their tiny town. My husband and I shared the kitchen with the entire household and the bathroom with another couple. Unfortunately, the bathroom didn't have a tub; the elderly couple who owned the house had taken it out and sold it for scrap after World War II. The water supply was from a cistern that collected rainwater from the rusty metal roof. I carried drinking water from a faucet across the street in a bucket. To do laundry, I'd have to drag a suitcase full of dirty clothes to the road, then flag down a bus to take me to the nearest town of any size.

The girl across the hall, Elsie, was much larger and more worldly-wise than I was. She told me that she had killed all the rats before we arrived, but that didn't make me feel any safer using the bathroom in the mornings. Elsie and I walked over to investigate any time we heard of any place to rent. The rental homes always turned *out to be chicken houses with a bare electric lightbulb hanging from the ceiling. The farmers would offer us a rake, a shovel, and a hose to make them livable! Times weren't easy then, but at least Elsie and I had each other to laugh with.*

When my husband shipped out, he found me a small apartment, again sight unseen, to live in, and this is where our first daughter, Sharon, and I lived. I didn't have a telephone, and the only heat was a two-burner hot plate. This is where I met my second guardian angel, the kind woman living across the street. She lent me a rocking chair. More than that, she'd let me use her phone in the evenings while she sat rocking my baby. Thanks to her, our nights were easier, and I didn't feel quite so alone.

Those early years were hard, but we made wonderful memories. Many kind people helped us through, and I wish I could thank each one. People who don't believe in guardian angels haven't met Southern women.

—Stella Malone
Alabama

Between Husbands

When I was young, "divorce" used to be a word spoken, if at all, in whispers. Although divorce is now much more common, we Southerners still believe in the sanctity of marriage, and divorce is not something that we take lightly. Unfortunately, it happens—in my case, four times.

No matter how common divorce becomes in the South, Southerners still have faith in the institution of marriage. No matter how many men we date who live with their mamas and dress like their granddads, who think that romance means giving us a set of Pyrex for our anniversaries, who can figure out how to tune up their car's engines, but think that a dirty diaper is an unsolvable mystery, we believe that men are wonderful in their hearts. We still have faith that, whatever happens, we'll find someone who is right to live with us throughout our days. I'm between husbands myself, though if you know any nice men, honey, I'm still looking.

Many of us regret, quite rightly, that marriages seem to end so quickly these days; it seems that spouses give up without giving every bit of energy that they can to the marriage. No sooner are we throwing rice as a friend drives off from her wedding than we're helping her look for a bachelorette apartment.

PEARL OF WISDOM

When a friend announces that she's divorcing, it's not the time to finally let her know how you really feel about that no-good, low-down, rotten man of hers. She and her husband may still have a chance to work out their differences, so don't add to her anger. And if, in spite of what you say, she and her husband reconcile, you probably won't be invited to the anniversary party.

When a friend divorces, she may find herself alone for the first time in years, if not the first time in her life. The best thing that you can do for a friend who is going through a divorce is to be there for her. No matter how unhappy she might have been with her husband, standing alone in the world takes some getting used to. With friends by her side, the transition will still be hard, but at least she'll have a friend by her side to lean on.

Keep in mind that divorce doesn't just affect your friends emotionally. A woman divorcing may find herself in the job market for the first time in years. She may suddenly need a babysitter for her children. She may never have managed her own finances, and she may not even have credit of her own. She may need to find an apartment or a smaller home. A Southern friend will keep all of these things in mind, and offer her friend help before she even asks. A little help can make a world of difference:

- If you have some simple accounting skills, help her to learn to manage her finances. There are several good computer software programs that can help make managing the bills, and the taxes, easy for someone who doesn't even know a credit card comes with a statement at the end of the month.
- Go along with your friend to search for an apartment or home, and if you have sewing or decorating skills, offer to help make that bachelorette pad a home.
- Offer to keep her kids for an evening or three. In difficult times, some women just want to be alone. A Southern mother will want to keep a positive face on for her children, but a few hours to just cry and get out her frustration can make a world of difference.

PEARL OF WISDOM

Some Southern men might have a slightly different take on divorce than Southern women. Says one good old boy: "She got the gold mine. I got the shaft. . . . They split it all down the middle, and then they gave her the better half. Well, I guess it all sounds funny . . . but it hurts too much to laugh. She got the gold mine. I got the shaft."—Jerry Reed, Georgia GRITS

Friendly Feuds

All girlfriends, even GRITS, eventually have their differences. Everyone has had a friend who has violated a confidence, destroyed trust by lying, or harmed you in some other way. Maybe you feel that your friend has insulted your children, your wardrobe, or your man, or maybe she feels that you have done the same. She may have told others about your veneers, face lift, or implants—not to mention the Botox! The fact is, even GRITS have their problems. The difference between Southern girls and other women is that when we disagree, we don't spread secrets about our friends all over town.

PEARL OF WISDOM

"Before you criticize someone, walk a mile in their shoes. That way, when you criticize them, you're a mile away and you have their shoes."
—*Ann Brashares*, Sisterhood of the Traveling Pants

Feelin' the Healin'

- *Let your friend know that you've been hurt. Now, I don't mean to yell and scream, and certainly not to call her names; my mother and yours taught us better than that. I do mean that you should say something like: "I felt hurt when you compared my backside to a semi and you said that my grandson looked like Michael Jackson on a bad morning." Let the feelings out, but do so without throwing accusations.*

- If you can, apologize to her for harboring your anger. Sometimes, just getting your thoughts out in the open can release the hurt and heal the friendship.
- Stay calm and be careful of what you say. Never burn a bridge. We've all said things that we regret later; when in doubt, keep your mouth shut.
- Don't dwell. We don't want others to sit stewing over our poor qualities (yes, even GRITS have a few), so we should show our friends the same courtesy. Think of all the things that made you friends in the first place. Then sit down and make a list of all the things that you like about her. You might even find yourself smiling and laughing, and realizing that the bad things are far outweighed by the good.
- Sometimes, just staying busy and staying away from each other works. When you're busy living your life, disagreements between friends tend to fall into the proper perspective.
- If you still have negative feelings, suggest a cooling-off period. Let your friend know that you don't have a problem with her; you just need to keep your distance for a while. If there needs to be blame, take it yourself.
- If you cannot heal the friendship, replace it with a positive one and learn from the experience. Never discuss the friendship ending with others, and never talk badly about an ex-husband, an ex-hairdresser, or an ex-friend. That's a rule every Southern girl's got to know.

No matter how much pain they feel in their hearts, Southern girls try to keep a positive face on for the world. We don't talk behind our friends' backs, just as we expect that they won't talk behind ours. When there's a feud between Southern girls, we like to keep it friendly. We just love killing them with kindness.

PEARL OF WISDOM

"Always forgive your enemies; nothing annoys them so much."
—Oscar Wilde

WELL, I DECLARE

In spite of their best efforts, even girls who were raised right find that they dwell on past wrongs. If you find that old hurts are as clear in your mind as the day they happened, the fault may be biological. Researchers at Wake Forest believe that when emotions run high— whether because of happiness or grief—the brain produces an enzyme, protein kinase C, that locks in long-term memory. This is why you may remember every detail of your first kiss, or your first breakup, even though you can't remember where you left your car keys.

PEARL OF WISDOM

Keep your friends close, but your enemies closer. We can always trust our friends, but I've learned from bitter experience that there are certain people who just don't have good in their hearts. GRITS know that one of the benefits to being ladylike, and treating those who treat us poorly civilly, is that we can keep an eye on them.

PEARL OF WISDOM

How to tell a friendship is in trouble:

- *You're back-stabbing instead of back-patting.*
- *You're taking ego trips instead of road trips.*
- *You're swapping insults instead of shoes.*
- *You're making judgment calls, not wake-up calls.*

When Friendship Goes South (I Mean North!)

Sometimes, no matter how hard we try, friendships simply don't make it. Not all women are GRITS, and even if they are, they sometimes grow apart. Most of the time, when a friendship ends, it's best to simply let it fade away. While it's sometimes best to be honest and explain your feelings, a dramatic ending to a relationship is usually not necessary. It's better to go out with style then to try to get in the last word. Besides, if you try to go out with a bang, you'll always just wish you'd said something more clever. That's just the way of the world, sugah.

PEARL OF WISDOM

After the Supremes broke up, their differences were aired in a very public, and very painful, way. "I have forgiven Mary. . . . But I no longer consider her a friend," wrote Diana Ross, referring to former Supreme Mary Wilson and her tell-all book Dreamgirl: My Life as a Supreme. *Dealing with Mary Wilson's book was a journey in which lightness triumphed over darkness. "I was depressed for a while," noted Diana, who sighed, "I had to allow our friendship to fade away."*
—Boze Hadleigh

So Long, Farewell, Auf Wiedersehen, Good-bye

If your friendship has these characteristics, it may be time to just let it go.

- *Lack of trust. You wouldn't give your friend your car keys, your dress size, or your lipstick, and she wouldn't give the same to you.*
- *Friendship is a low priority. If you could see your friend but, well, that repeat of Jeopardy is on again, you may want to reconsider her role in your life.*
- *Jealousy and competitiveness. If you get married, but she takes a honeymoon; if your child wins a track meet, and she hires a private Olympic trainer for hers; if you buy a pickup, and she buys a monster truck, you might want to reconsider the friendship.*
- *Broken promises and shared secrets. A woman who would tell the world that you wear a girdle is not a friend.*
- *The friendship is a duty, not an enjoyment. Face it, you wouldn't want to spend hours with your mother-in-law. Why spend time with a friend who just feels like one?*
- *Unequal giving and taking. If you've painted her bedroom, baby-sat for her children, and listened to her whine for two hours about her boss, yet she can't take a few minutes to talk about your marriage, you may need to find a new friend.*

We Southern girls often will hang on to friendships long after they've become unrewarding or even destructive. Our mothers taught us to always be friendly, and that's advice I agree with. But sometimes we take that advice to mean that we always need to be friends. Sometimes, it takes more strength to let go than it takes to hang on. If a friendship is past salvaging, don't be afraid to step back and say, "No more." We'll always be friendly, we'll always be ladylike, and we'll be smiling as we walk on out the door.

Ex-Rated Problems

Unfortunately, we all have an ex or two to deal with in our lives.

- *When an ex-boyfriend or ex-husband finds someone new, always try to be friendly, especially if there are children involved. Still, just because you're friendly doesn't mean that you have to be friends. There's a story going around about a mother of the bride who has to deal with her ex-husband's aggressive and competitive new wife. The new wife chooses the same dress as the mother of the bride for the wedding, a dress the mother has already purchased, but the new wife won't back down. The mother agrees to wear a different dress to the wedding, and she remains pleasant and calm. When her daughter asks her how she can have such a good attitude, the mother says: "Don't worry, sweetheart, this dress will be perfect for the rehearsal dinner."*
- *If you've lost your job, you may be forced to have business dealings or socialize with your ex-boss and co-workers. Never spread blame, and never bad-mouth your company. If someone asks you what happened, a simple "I lost my job" or "Things just didn't work out" is always preferable to "My boss has no more sense than a baboon and his toupee looks like a dead*

possum." You may have to work with them again, and you want it to be on the best terms possible. Not only will you look good in their eyes, but potential employers will notice and appreciate your attitude.

- If you have ex-friends, keep your problems between the two of you. No one needs to even know that the friendship is gone; it's a private matter. Taking the high road might be difficult, especially if she doesn't show you the same courtesy, but in the end you'll feel better and look better to those around you. You might get some satisfaction in the short term by dishing the dirt about your ex-friend, but in the long term, no matter how much she might deserve what you say, people will remember you as the one who told tales.

- Your ex-roommate may lounge on the couch all day in a ratty old bathrobe, drink straight from the milk carton, and juggle dates with two men at the same time, but keep her secrets to yourself. There are some moments in a Southern girl's life that are best kept quiet. If you're tempted to tell the world that she still sleeps with her teddy bear, remember: Would you like it if your ex-roommate told the world how many of your hairs wind up in the shower drain or about all the different ointments in your medicine cabinet?

CHAPTER 12

Men Come and Go, But a Friend Is Forevah

"I never married because there was no need. I have three pets at home that answer the same purpose as a husband. I have a dog that growls every morning, a parrot that swears every afternoon, and a cat that comes home late at night."—MARIE CORELLI

"P.S. It's all gossip about the prince. I'm not in the habit of taking my girlfriends' beaux."—*WALLIS WARFIELD*, the American-born Duchess of Windsor, but not a GRITS. The prince in question, King Edward, later abdicated the British throne to marry her.

When people think of Southern women, the image of Scarlett O'Hara comes to mind. The men tripped over their own feet trying to bring her a dessert or a fan, and the women tripped over their feet trying to get away from her. Scarlett had no use for women, and women had no use for her.

Now, there are plenty of women who would throw their women friends over at the first sight of a handsome man and, I'm sad to say, some of them are even Southern women. True GRITS wouldn't dream of giving up the women in their lives for men; they know that men might come and go, but friends are forevah! Southern women find men together, flirt together, and stand by their friends' sides at weddings and divorces. They complain about their men, bless their hearts, and share the fun and frustrations of boyfriends and husbands. For GRITS, men can be another reason to love your girlfriends.

Dating Dos

- Many women on the shady side of fifty are single for the first time. Maybe their marriages have ended because the children finally moved out of the house, or maybe their dear husbands have passed away. Whatever the reason, women of a certain age can flirt and date with the best of them. Don't be afraid to ask your girlfriends for help. Your girlfriends can guide you through every aspect of dating, from how to dress to how to say good night at the end of the evening. More important, they can tell you how wonderful you are and how any man would be lucky to have you, and they'll actually mean what they say.

- If you still don't have a date, don't be afraid to ask your girlfriends to help set you up. No one can play matchmaker like a GRITS! Dating can be as uncomfortable as a tight corset at first, so don't expect things to go smoothly. Remember, honey, dating is awkward for twenty-two-year-olds, too. So relax, try to have a good time, and enjoy a new adventure.

- Watching our daughters and granddaughters start dating often feels like handing over our most precious family heirlooms to a teamster. If she's a teenager, encourage your daughter to bring young men home to meet you before she dates them, and don't be afraid to forbid her to date someone who is inappropriate. She might whine and roll her eyes at your old-timey ways, but deep down, she appreciates the fact that you care. If she's an adult, and she decides to date a young man whom you don't approve of, don't nag her about him. If he isn't right for her, and you've raised her right, she'll figure it out for herself. Disapproving words may only drive the star-crossed lovers together, and if you hold your tongue, you may find that the relationship ends faster.

- If you're married or in a relationship, don't neglect your friends. A minister once told me that his parishioners with the best marriages had two things in common: a strong relationship with God, and a strong relationship with friends. You may be busy keeping up a house and keeping up a man, but take time out to appreciate your friends. If you can, set aside an afternoon or an evening each week when you can have a meal with your girlfriends, watch those sappy old movies, and gossip like teenagers without bothering the men in your lives. Encourage him to go out with the boys; after all, it's a great opportunity to get that love of monster trucks out of his system. The time that you spend with your girlfriends will make the time that you spend with the man in your life even better.

- Those times when you're between relationships with men may be lonely, but they're also a wonderful time to learn about the most important person in your life: you! Take the opportunity to read about something that's always interested you, to volunteer for a cause you feel passionate about, or to start a new hobby. You'll learn what drives you, you'll feel that you're doing something valuable with your life, and you'll have the opportunity to meet new people—male and female.

Don't make the mistake of thinking all of us single girls are pining by the phone every night, waiting for some man to call. Most of us know that life is for the living, man or no man. Even if some of us are sitting by the phone, the difference between GRITS and other women is that we don't shout it out to the whole world; we tell only our closest friends.

A lot of women, GRITS or not, go through times of loneliness. Even with all my friends, I sometimes feel alone, but I know that loneliness isn't always a bad thing. I've talked with many of my girlfriends about loneliness, and we've found that those times when we were most lonely were often the times when we've grown the most as people. We can learn in these times how strong we are, and what is really important to us.

GRITS know that they should reach out to anyone, GRITS or not, who seems to be lonely. Not only can you help someone else, you'll be helping yourself to gain a new friend. Goodness knows, with GRITS for friends, we don't ever have to be alone.

We're with our girlfriends for work, for worship, and for tearing up the town. By picking up the phone or poking our heads into the next room, we've got someone to take to the movies, to shop with us, or just to watch a silly old romantic movie with. We consult our girlfriends about everything from what apartment to rent to what shade of nail polish looks best with our skin. Girlfriends help us to stand on our own, to show our bosses what we're made of, and to show no-good men the door. Girls give us support, sisterhood, and a bit of spine. Men are wonderful, but we know that we can count on our girlfriends through everything life brings.

WELL, I DECLARE

Do you sometimes think the man in your life is going to drive you crazy? You're probably right, sugar. According to British researchers, women who stay single are much more likely to have better mental health than women who have been in long-term relationships, but, then again, they were dating British men, not good old Southern boys.

If you need to talk to someone in the middle of the night, your husband will probably just mutter something in his sleep and roll over to snore for a few more hours. Your girlfriend will sit up and demand that you spill all the details. Your girlfriends will stand by your side through bad jobs, bad men, and even bad hair. They'll help you mop up a flooded basement, they'll run out to the middle of nowhere to put gas in your car, or they'll help you mend a broken heart.

GRITS GLOSSARY

Bevy of beauties [be-vee əv byoo-teez] n. *Any group of unmarried Southern girls. Whether they are young or ripe with maturity, and whether their clothes are from a boutique or the thrift store, whenever you have two or more Southern girlfriends, a bevy of beauties is found.*

In a lot of ways, being single with a few good girlfriends can be a lot better than being married. Sure, your girlfriends won't buy you flowers or open doors for you, but your man probably didn't, either. And your girlfriends will help you out in ways that matter a whole lot more. Your girlfriends don't care if you pack on a few extra pounds, though they'll sure be happy to help you lose them. When someone volunteers you to bake four dozen brownies for the church bake sale, your girlfriends will be right by your side in the kitchen. When your child has gum in his hair, as well as the peanut butter and shortening that you used to try to get it out, your girlfriend will help you play barber. When you have a big date, your girlfriend will help you pick your best dress, and she'll be honest about whether you have panty lines. When your living room is the victim of a Superbowl party, your girlfriend will stay until every speck of dirt is gone.

WELL, I DECLARE

According to the U.S. Census Bureau, about forty-three percent of Americans over the age of fifteen are unmarried. New York has the highest percentage of unmarried people, at fifty percent. No Southerner would be surprised. After all, who in their right mind would marry a New Yorker?

GRITS in the City

Staying home with your girlfriends is fun, but getting out with your girlfriends to paint the town red is even better! If Southern girls make hearts go a mile a minute, a whole gaggle of them can just about fill an emergency room. When Southern girls go out on the town, they travel in packs. Some people think it's because we love the security of groups. Some people think it's that we want to make a big impact. Some people think it's because we just love to make a lot of noise. I know the real reason, though: We just can't get enough of our girlfriends.

PEARL OF WISDOM

I have a male friend who says that if they want to find Jimmy Hoffa's body, they just need to look in a Southern girl's pocketbook. We Southern girls pack everything from afternoon snacks to Rolodexes in our bags, but an evening out is a chance to go light. Your outfit will look better, and you won't have a big clumsy thing to lug around, if you carry a small clutch with a license, a credit card, a few dollars, and a lipstick. If you're left holding your girlfriend's bag, remember not to peek into it: A Southern girl's pocketbook is sacred!

GRITS love luxury, and they have taste, but it isn't the velvet ropes of exclusive nightclubs that make a Southern girl happy. She doesn't care if you're an Astor on Park Avenue or a McCoy up in the hills. She would rather have a Southern girl with a warm heart and a warm smile for a friend than a wealthy socialite with millions in the bank. When they go out to paint the town, GRITS are happier in a honky tonk with their friends than they would be in a cold, hoity-toity club with strangers.

The fact is, any place full of GRITS is the place to be. Whether they live in glitzy and fast Houston or quiet and relaxed Johnson City, GRITS know that their girlfriends make any place the "in" place. A Southern girl might be in a church basement, a country club, a restaurant, a charity ball, a football game, or just a friend's backyard; it's her smile, her laugh, and her stunning good looks that make being around her so wonderful.

It's nice to impress the men, and goodness knows that we

do, but it's a lot more important that we have fun with our friends. We love batting our eyelashes and swishing back our long hair, but it's laughing with our girlfriends that really makes us happy. Still, even impressing the boys is something that we Southern girls can do together.

Flirting, in a ladylike way, of course, can be a group activity. Your girlfriends can draw your eyes to that quiet, handsome man in the corner that you might never have noticed otherwise, and they can also point out the nose hair and the smarmy smile on the man who was so good-looking at first glance. Girlfriends can gently talk about your good looks to men who might not have paid you any notice otherwise, and they can rescue you from the ones you'd rather hadn't.

If you and your girlfriends are going to show your charms to the men of the world, keep a few simple rules in mind.

- *As much as you love your girlfriends, try to keep your group small. The beauty of all you Southern belles together might just scare all but the most hardy, or obnoxious, souls away.*
- *Keep your sipping to a minimum or, better yet, drink something nonalcoholic. Your skin will stay fresh, your lipstick will look nice, and you won't give your number to that guy in the plaid pants who still lives with his mother.*
- *Whatever you do, sugar, don't smoke! It's hard to look like a lady when you smell like an ashtray. If you must smoke— frankly, I don't think a well-brought-up woman ever should— please behave like a lady.*
- *There might be a lot of men at bars, but you and your girlfriends are more likely to meet men you respect at places where there's no*

drinking. Besides, when you bring the perfect man home to Mother, or to your grown children, would you rather say that you met at Tipsy McGiggle's Bar or a church outing?

- By all means, never chew gum in public. If for some reason you can't stop yourself, don't talk while chewing. A man wants to date a lady, not a cow chewing her cud.

- Have a signal you can send your girlfriends in case you get trapped in a conversation with a taxidermist whose sole topic of conversation is his ex-wife—and you're not entirely sure he didn't have her stuffed and mounted. Be sure that it's noticeable but subtle; although patting the top of your head while waving your free hand will get your girlfriends' attention, or at least scare away a pest, it will also make every other person in the room think you're teched.

- Don't get so caught up in getting a man's number that you abandon your friends. Remember, men come and go, but your girlfriends are there for life.

PEARL OF WISDOM

My friends and I have a pact not to evah, evah date the ex-boyfriend or ex-husband of a girlfriend. Whether our friends have moved to the next county or even to the next world, we won't evah touch each other's men!

A great thing about girlfriends is that you don't have to go out and show yourself off all over town to get a date; any Southern woman worth her white gloves loves to play matchmaker. Now, sometimes this means that your Aunt Gertie is going to set you up with an accountant who can, and will, debate the merits of various lawn fertilizers for an hour, but sometimes it means that your best girlfriend will set you up with a jazz singer who spends his free time volunteering at a soup kitchen. Sure, blind dates can be unfortunate, but your friends know you far better than strangers at some singles bar, and sometimes it's nice to put yourself in their hands. Besides, what have you got to lose besides a night watching reruns on the television?

Ramblings of a Hopeful Cynic

You know when you watch a great movie, where the guy gets the girl and everything ends up happily ever after, you turn to your friend and say: "Nothing like that ever happens in real life." Why is that, I wonder?

Well, in the movies, when the main character jumps on a plane to see a guy she hardly knows but knows she can hardly live without, her best friend is always in the terminal yelling: "Good luck! Call me!" In real life, people are too caught up in lawsuits and personal responsibility to yell anything but: "Have you considered all the probable outcomes of this course of action and weighed the pros and cons adequately to insure prevention of probable harm to ego and emotion?"

I think it's time for best friends to step up to the plate and yell: "Good luck! If you're not having too much fun to remember I exist, call me!" If the world falls apart on the way home, at least you have an excuse to move on and share a gallon of rocky road with your best friend. If you're going to end up alone, at least you should have a darned good time getting there!

—Corey Kirkland
Eufaula, Alabama

Can This Marriage Be Stopped?

We've all had it happen. A soft-spoken, well-dressed, attractive friend is suddenly dating a man who chews tobacco, tells inappropriate jokes at the top of his lungs . . . in church, and thinks a romantic date is a TV dinner heated up by his "old lady." You bide your time, hoping that he'll go away, and when you get a call late at night from your friend, breathless and weeping, you think with relief that it's finally over . . . until she announces that she's engaged.

The fact is, even Southern women date and marry men who are simply not appropriate. They might think that he's a good-looking bad boy. They might think that he'll change his ways. They might just think that they'll never find a man who measures up to their expectations. Or they just might be that desperate. Whatever the reason, sometimes, when a friend says that she's marrying the man of her dreams, it's a nightmare.

When Beauty Meets the Beast

- *It's easier to be with a difficult person if you surround yourself with buffers. Rather than asking your friend and her fiancé over for a quiet dinner, try having a big barbecue for all of your friends.*
- *Be honest with yourself: Do you want your friend to leave him because he's wrong for her, or because you don't like him? After all, you're not the one who's going to spend the rest of your life with his snoring body by your side and his smelly old hound dog nestled by your feet.*

- *Get to know him on his own terms. If your circle spends its time sipping chardonnay and listening to symphonies, and his circle swigs bourbon and listens to Willie Nelson, or vice versa, he may be disagreeable because he's uncomfortable. Find out his interests from your friend, and when you get together, do something that puts him more at ease.*
- *If all else fails, you aren't dating him. Keep inviting your friend out for girls' nights, for shopping, for whatever you did together before she met her man. Skip the dinner parties and couples' nights. While it isn't a good idea to tell your friend that her boyfriend is not invited, it is a good idea to tell her how much you like her, and how much you treasure her friendship. Tell her that you want to spend some time with her, not that you want to avoid him.*

Most of the time, when a friend is with a man you don't like, it's better to bite your tongue. Of course, if he's abusing her, and you think that she's with him out of fear, no true friend will sit by quietly. Most of the time, though, it's better to remember that your friend is a grown-up, and she's just going to have to make her own mistakes. If you share your real feelings about her man, you may open her eyes but, most likely, you'll just lose a friend.

Remember: You can lead a horse to water, but you can't make him drink. For men, maybe that rule should be: You can lead a man to water, but you can't make him think! We Southern women love to take care of others, and sometimes we make the mistake of thinking that we can change the men in our lives once they're our boyfriends or husbands. You can show a man how to act properly, but it's unlikely that you'll change his ways greatly. Love him for who he is, or move on to some other horse.

I've heard all my life from other GRITS: "Don't worry, honey. Men are like buses—there will always be another one at the next corner!"

Bridesmaids

It's possible for Southern girls to live single and happy for their whole lives, and more of them are doing it these days. For a traditional Southern girl, though, no date is more important than her wedding, whether it's her first or her fourth. Without her girlfriends by her side, a wedding just would not be the same. GRITS have been known to go a bit overboard with our bridesmaids, at least according to our husbands and daddies. They just don't understand why any girl in her right mind would want twelve of her friends standing by her side at the church. We know that it's not because we want to make a bigger splash than that obnoxious Lulu down the block; it's because we want to share the most important moment of our lives with our best friends.

PEARL OF WISDOM

Every woman, whether she's nineteen or ninety, deserves to wear the dress of her dreams to her wedding. If you want an elegant gown in pure white, sugar, by all means, go out and buy it. You might look a little funny in a full-length white dress when your granddaughter is your flower girl, but it's your day, and you deserve for it to live up to your fantasies.

Ya-Ya Bridesmaid Brunch

My friends and I have been through everything together since we were eight years old. There are five of us "Ya-Yas," and we still get together for what we call "Retreats," though sometimes only three or four of us can make it. When all five of us, Gracie, Jules, Jane, Mary, and Sherry, are there, watch out!

None of us live in the same city and only three of us live in Alabama, but for the thirty years since we've graduated from college, we've managed to get together every year.

Between us, we have ten daughters, or "Petite Ya-Yas." When Gracie's oldest girl decided to get married, it was up to me to throw a bridal shower. Jane was across the waters and Jules was otherwise occupied, so that left me, Sherry, and our Yankee Ya-Ya, Mary. Since our three families have been intertwined for forty years, we decided to do a Ya-Ya Bridesmaid Brunch, incorporating elements from our families' lives, at the home of the bride. We wanted the Petites to know just how important girlfriends are.

Mary and I put our heads together, and we managed to bring pieces of all our families to the entertaining. We set a traditional pink bridesmaid's cake with a thimble in it on a pink Depression glass cake *plate that belonged to my grandmother. We gathered silver, china, crystal, table linens, and vases from the three of us, our three mothers, and our three grandmothers. Every table was set with something from each of the three families.*

We presented the bride with a silver tray with her new surname and the names of all the Ya-Yas engraved on the front, and another tradition was born. We have now had two of our girl Petites marry, and both had a Ya-Ya Bridesmaid Brunch. Marriage is about combining families and traditions, and it just wouldn't be the same without friends by your side.

—Sherry Campbell
—Grace Hill
—Mary Haslit
—Julianne Parris
—Jane Thatcher
 Alabama

Even though the wedding day means the end of single life, it doesn't mean the end of those friendships that we built during those years. We like our friends to be our bridesmaids because we know that we aren't giving those friendships up; we're taking them with us into our new lives. When a bride asks her girlfriend to be a bridesmaid, she's telling her that she's special enough to share her most precious day.

WELL, I DECLARE

In the antebellum South, a bride usually did not wear white at her wedding, but her bridesmaids often did. However, at the wedding of Martha "Mittie" Bulloch and Theodore Roosevelt, Sr., in Georgia in 1853, both the bridesmaids and the bride wore white. Mittie wore a white silk gown with an illusion veil that covered the full length of her train. She carried a small prayer book rather than flowers. Her bridesmaids wore white muslin gowns and carried evergreen branches.

Bridesmaids watch out for the bride when her mind is occupied with everything from whether the florist will show up on time to whether her mother is going to make a snippy comment to her father's new wife. They make sure her dress is straight and she has no lipstick on her teeth. Bridesmaids assure the bride that no matter what the groom and best man got up to last night, nothing in the world would make her dear beau late for the ceremony. Bridesmaids always have an extra tissue for clumping mascara and falling tears. Bridesmaids hold her hand, tell her everything will be fine, and fetch a ginger ale for that queasy stomach. Most of all, bridesmaids stand by the bride's side and tell her she's the most beautiful bride they've ever seen.

GRITS GLOSSARY

Jumping the broom [jump-ing thə broom] n. *An African-American wedding tradition. Before the Civil War, slave owners sought to deprive their slaves of the basic dignity of marriage, so Southern slaves used the tradition of jumping a broom to formalize weddings. Many black Southerners incorporate this custom into their modern weddings as a way of honoring their heritage.*

As much an honor as it is to be a bridesmaid, sometimes we Southern girls would rather be spared the privilege. Buying a big, poofy chartreuse dress, sitting through an interminable rehearsal, and walking down the aisle with a smile on your face while yet another of your friends snaps up a gorgeous Southern bachelor isn't every girl's idea of a dream weekend. Still, we GRITS are willing to put up with uncomfortable dyed shoes for the sake of our girlfriends and making their magic day everything they've dreamed about.

Myrtle the Girdle

Will and Alyssa were married on a glorious October night in a storybook wedding for a storybook couple. I had introduced them five years ago, and they had asked me to read the scripture during their wedding. I read with sincere love of God and of the couple.

A few hours later, for reasons that can only be explained by champagne and the adrenaline of dancing, I decided to join a group of rowdy bridesmaids at the Tap Room, our favorite college hole-in-the-wall. On the way there, I decided to lose the girdle that I had been wearing to fit into the skirt that was at least two sizes too small for me. I tucked the girdle as discreetly as I could into the cocktail-sized purse I'd been carrying.

I placed the purse next to our table and left it to go talk to friends. Little did I know that our group at the table was soon replaced by strangers. An hour later, I looked up to see the girdle being thrown around the Tap Room. When I saw an old friend pull it over his head, my fight-or-flight reaction kicked in, and you can bet I flew! I ran outside, followed by the bridesmaids.

They managed to calm me down a bit, and made me believe that no one knew the girdle was mine. Unfortunately, they couldn't be more wrong. The first man to hurtle the girdle later explained to me that the strangers at our table asked who owned the purse. In searching for an ID, he found Myrtle the Girdle. He said that he didn't know what got into him, but he sent that girdle flying. He apologized from the bottom of his heart, and I guess I forgive him. Maybe he did make Myrtle the Girdle a legend at the Tap Room.

—Laura Lefler
Loudon, Tennessee

As hard as being a bridesmaid is sometimes, it helps to look at the bright side. Sure, you probably won't be wearing the lavender taffeta monstrosity to next year's Christmas party, but being a bridesmaid is not about how you look. It's about standing by the side of a wonderful Southern girlfriend as she marries a fabulous Southern gentleman. So take a sip of champagne, bat your eyelashes at that good-looking usher, and have a wonderful time.

It's Not Raining Men

No matter how well-dressed, how charming, and how shining their smiles, even GRITS have dry spells with men. Your last date may have been when bellbottoms were high fashion . . . for the first time. If it isn't raining men, if there isn't even a cloud on the horizon, hard work is called for.

- *Putting yourself out in public, and letting as many men and women see you as possible, is the only way to get noticed.*

Classes, work, clubs, and church are not only good for the spirit and the soul, they're great ways to meet people. Sitting around in your sweatpants eating microwave popcorn may be a comfortable way to spend the evening, but it won't help you meet new people, and it's certainly doing no favors for your thighs. Being in new social situations is never comfortable for anyone, but when you meet new friends, and maybe even the man of your dreams, it will be worth it.

- If you're looking for a man, don't be too shy to let your girlfriends know it. It's possible to meet a wonderful man on your own, but with all your GRITS girlfriends looking for you, you can't lose.

- Take time to care for your appearance and for your spirit. First impressions are important to everyone, but especially to men because, let's face it, they're a little shallow. If you are a nurturing woman with a good sense of humor, for goodness' sake, sugar, don't hide it behind a frumpy dress and frizzy hair! Keep your hair, your makeup, and your clothes in order anytime you leave the house, and take care of your health with exercise and healthy food. You don't have to be a supermodel—most men don't want those twig-thin fashion victims anyway—just do the best with what you have. The better you look, the better you'll feel, and when you feel good, you'll stand tall, smile broadly, and get the attention of every man in the room.

- Most important, remember that men aren't everything. You have to love yourself to inspire others to love you. Live your life fully, take joy in what you have, and you may find that the happiness and self-confidence you feel will attract a man when you least expect it.

CHAPTER 13

Growing Better Together

"Sure I'm for helping the elderly. I'm going to be old myself someday."—LILLIAN CARTER, GEORGIA, SPOKEN IN HER EIGHTIES

"The fear of death follows from the fear of life. A man who lives fully is prepared to die at any time."—MARK TWAIN, MISSOURI GRITS

GRITS don't grow old, and they certainly don't fade away; they grow better each day. We might gain a few pounds around the middle, lose a few inches from the top, and find hairs in places we never expected, but we're still the GRITS we always were.

As we grow better, our girlfriends are more important than ever. We need our girlfriends to keep us sharp and active and, of course, so that we can have someone to share stories of our grandchildren with (it's not bragging if it's true, sugar). Maturity is a time for exploring life anew, for learning and growing in ways we never could when we were chasing after children and holding down a job. It is also a time for illness and death, and our girlfriends are there to listen to our tears, and to share a laugh with us when we're ready to start living again.

The Best Years of Our Lives

- If a friend has to enter an assisted-living facility or nursing home, she may feel that her life is over. Prove her wrong! Visit her as often as possible, and encourage your other friends to do the same. When you visit, don't bring the standard flowers;

bring books, tapes, puzzles, magazines, and pictures to keep her mind occupied and active. If you can, try to get her out in a public area. If you can start a three-way conversation with another resident, when you leave, your friend may have a new friend to keep her company.

- When the kids have moved on, and you've said good-bye to a nine-to-five job, it's the perfect time to explore our beautiful country, and even the world. Laura Bush schedules regular trips with her girlfriends from Midland, Texas. They celebrated their fortieth birthdays with a trip to the Grand Canyon, and their fiftieth on the Yampa River. If the first lady can find the time to travel with her girlfriends, so can those of us who are just queens of our double-wide trailers. Growing up shouldn't mean growing moss, so grab your girlfriends and hit the road.

- You are never too old to try something new. Try a new color of nail polish, and don't worry if it's too flashy for someone your age. Learn to play a new sport, and keep your body and mind active. Cook up something new and spicy, whether it's in the kitchen or with your husband in another room. And whatever new thing you try, challenge your girlfriends to do it, too. Girlfriends give you the courage to step out of your routine, and they make whatever you're doing more fun. Age isn't about how many years you've lived; it's about your attitude. I, for one, plan to be young for years to come, and I plan on having my GRITS girlfriends growing young right beside me.

Spending Your Children's Inheritance

It's the middle of the afternoon, and there's a strange man in your living room. He's wearing shorts and black kneesocks, and he's starting to doze in the La-Z-Boy. You stare at that strange creature for a few minutes before you realize that he's a bit familiar: That strange man is your husband.

Whether you've finally gotten a gold watch and a pension yourself, or your husband is getting his, retirement can be a strange time in a Southern girl's life. Just when you've finally gotten used to your routine, sending your husband off to meet the day with a kiss, or traveling in the carpool yourself, you have to get used to something else entirely.

PEARL OF WISDOM

Mothers never retire from their jobs, but they sometimes get a new and better one: grandchildren. It's a job women, and especially Southern women, wouldn't trade for seats in any boardroom. Says Ann Bowden, wife of Florida State coach Bobby Bowden: "My home is my stadium, and my grandchildren are my players."

Retirement is a time to reconnect with an old friend, and this time, it's not a woman. It's a wonderful opportunity to become friends with the man you married, to rediscover why you love each other, and to explore a new phase in life together.

WELL, I DECLARE

We all know that we have to exercise our bodies to maintain health, but researchers now say that the same may be true of our brains. Activities that keep you mentally active may offer some protection against Alzheimer's disease. Playing bridge is a way not only of meeting new girlfriends, and gossiping about your husbands, but it is also a wonderful way to maintain your brain.

Retirement is also a time to reconnect with your old girlfriends and to make new ones. Face it, even if your marriage is still music and roses after retirement, even twenty-four hours of uninterrupted romance will get on your last nerve after a while. Girlfriends can take the pressure off of your marriage by giving you some time to be just one of the girls.

Fun After Fifty-Five

- *We'd all love to explore the finest European hotels and cruise the Caribbean in our retirement years, but for many of us, retirement means adjusting to a fixed income. One way to travel on a budget is to take advantage of elder hostels. Elder hostels promote lifelong learning, whether you want to learn about the Louvre or Lafayette, and they're a wonderful way to meet other mature people who take an interest in life.*
- *Joining a group of women who're on the right side of fifty, such as the Red Hat Society, can keep your spirits in the right place. When your thighs are so big they have their own Zip code and you find that your mustache is thicker than your*

husband's, a group of women in the same boat as you can keep you laughing at your problems.

- For many people, retirement can be a time of loneliness, especially for those of us who wake up by ourselves each morning. One way to combat loneliness is to find a strong purpose in life, a way to give of yourself. Fortunately, our communities need you to volunteer as much as you need to keep active. If you love books or children, volunteer at your local library. If you love animals, shelters always need people to clean the cages and walk the animals. Giving to others is one of the best ways to enjoy life and to stay healthy. I know of a couple in their late eighties who go out to deliver Meals on Wheels to the homebound. The joy they feel in helping others—many of whom are twenty years younger than they are—helps to keep them young.

- Reconnect with old friends. Ever wonder what happened to your best friend from elementary school? What about that sorority sister who helped you through some of the worst patches of your young life? Well, you've finally got the time to track them down. I can guarantee that they'll be tickled pink to hear from you. You know I can't say it enough: Friends really are forevah.

- You've spent a lifetime taking care of others, so take some time to take care of yourself. Don't think that your days as a bombshell are over just because of a few crow's-feet or a soft tummy; you can be fabulous at fifty, sixty, and beyond. A large part of beauty comes from within, and in my mind, a seventy-year-old who stands tall and shines is more beautiful than a forty-year-old who sulks and slouches.

There's a change that binds all women together: the change of life. Professional or homemaker, childless or mother of twelve, high-style or down-home, we all go through it. There was a day when a well-brought-up woman would blush at the thought of discussing "the change." Southern girls still don't shout about hormone replacement to the neighbors, but they aren't afraid to get the support they need from their close girlfriends.

Menopause doesn't have to be a bad thing. Some of us have the hot flashes, the night sweats, and the hormone crazies that send the men in our lives running for cover, and some of us sail through with no symptoms at all. Menopause doesn't make us any less feminine; it just makes us women with more experience. Southern women love their children, of course, but it is also a relief to know that we never have to be mommies again; now the time has come instead to start pestering those daughters to give us grandchildren.

PEARL OF WISDOM

"I refuse to think of them as chin hairs. I think of them as stray eyebrows."—Janette Barber (Sometimes even New York comedians can have a belle's attitude.)

Men blame sports cars, girlfriends, and unfortunate ear piercings on their midlife crises, so go ahead and have a little fun with your change in life. Do something that you always wanted to do, but you thought you never could. Grab a girlfriend's hand and take that cruise to Cancún. Buy yourself that gorgeous diamond tennis bracelet. Flip your hair and bat your eyelashes at that handsome, newly single doctor. Turn menopause into the pause that refreshes. After all, none of us is getting any younger, so we might as well have some fun.

PEARL OF WISDOM

Some people believe that women of a certain age should wear longer skirts, darker colors, and shorter hair. I say, forget that, sugar! Dress in a way that makes you comfortable, and if that means flaunting what you have, why, go ahead. You're never too old to be a belle.

It Ain't All Thorns

An old mountain woman, Aunt Airy, when asked about living alone at her advanced age, said, "It ain't all roses and it ain't all thorns." That's how it is for my family now that I'm past seventy-five, but there are still more roses than thorns.

There are a few problems I consider thorns. I encounter a little stiffness and a few creaks in the mornings. I don't have as much stamina as I did when I was younger, and I can no longer do justice to "All You Can Eat" buffets. Someone has stolen most of the names in my memory. Between my husband and I, we have as many doctors as Heinz has varieties.

Those pesky things are nothing compared to the abundance of roses. I'll never have to go to another PTA meeting, be a room mother, or suffer with a Scout troop trying to build a fire with nothing but damp green pine logs again. I was clubbed to death by the time I was forty, and I'll never have to attend a committee or club meeting again.

As much as I like old hens individually, a bunch of them together can be traumatic.

My husband and I have noticed lately that our son and daughter have grown quite wise and can even give us advice on occasion. We've known our daughter-in-law and son-in-law so long that they feel like our own children, and knowing them is pleasant and fulfilling. After years of responsibilities, we now have few and are able to enjoy our five grandchildren. They range in age from fifteen to twenty-seven, and there's no generation gap. After years of handing out advice, the "grands" are teaching us. We're on to Walkmans, blow-dryers, and CDs. They've become not just grandchildren, but wonderful friends. A sound about as thrilling as a new CD is when the phone rings about once a week and one of the five says, "Hey, are y'all busy this weekend? I want to come hang out with you."

Perhaps a marriage of fifty-five years is the best rose of all. The good times have made our love more intense, and the hard times have made us stronger. The years have made our disagreements more rare; we need only a few to keep ourselves sharp. We'd be a colorless pair of old dummies if we'd shared only one opinion all these years. Our relationship is more comfortable, yet more exciting, like putting on a soft warm robe on a cool morning and standing in front of the fire. As we count our blessings and relive happy memories, we look forward each morning to a joyous day. Of course, every day doesn't come up roses, but I'll tell the world it's a heck of a lot more fun to be young in an old body than old in a young one, and it ain't all thorns.

—Mary Dozier Thomas
Eufaula, Alabama

Since the change comes to all of us eventually, there's never a shortage of women friends to talk with. For women who go through the change earlier—it happens even to women in their thirties—it may be necessary to reach out to an older relative or friend, but eventually, honey, we're all going to be in the same place. We all get to the point when we're cruising down the road in our cars, and we can't remember for the life of us where we're going. We reach the day when every little nibble of Aunt Wanda's fried pies heads straight for our thighs. No matter how much we struggle against it, we're all going to sag in all the wrong places that used to be so right. All we can do is talk to our friends, laugh, and realize that we can get through these times only if we do it together. Besides, I like to think that, if our waistlines and rears are expanding, it must be because they're so filled with love!

PEARL OF WISDOM

A reporter, when interviewing a 104-year-old woman: "What is the best thing about being 104?"
She replied, "No peer pressure."
—Sylvia R. Shiner

Creaks and Cranks

There comes a point in every woman's life when she realizes that that strange creaking sound she hears every time she walks across the floor isn't a loose board, it's her. Southern women don't like to complain about themselves, but on those mornings when your joints are stiff, your back is sore, and you have aches in body parts you didn't know you had, it's hard not to let that whine flow freely.

Maturity brings with it wisdom and judgment but, unfortunately, it also brings a mature body. It seems unfair that just as we're learning to really let loose and enjoy life, our bodies start to betray us, but GRITS know that the only way to handle life's problems is with strength. Having our families and our girlfriends beside us can help; they're going through the same thing that we are, and they can keep us smiling, even though we know that those smile lines aren't getting any shallower.

Nursing Home Cafeteria

I sit next to my mother at the lunch table in her nursing home, as I do every week (she claims I only come once a month). She holds her head in her hands and won't look up.

"Mother, do you want me to play piano? I brought my books."

"Do what you want to do."

"Do you want to stroll around before lunch?"

"Noooo."

"It's a beautiful day outside. Do you want to go for a drive?"

"I can't go outside. I ain't able."

"Mother, I brought you an apple. Do you want some?"

"I don't want no damn apple." I cut a small piece and peel it. She takes it and eats it, never lifting her head from her hands.

"Do you want me to play?"

"Well, if you're going to, quit assing around and be done with it."

I sit down at the piano next to her. I start with a Patsy Cline song. Some of the residents even applaud. Then I move to a couple of Bob Dylan songs. I only know five songs, so it doesn't take too long for me to finish my whole repertoire.

With lunch over, Mother is ready to go. A couple of wheelchairs are blocking the door. Mother shouts at them to get out of the way. "Go around them if they can't move it," she orders me.

I push her back to the hall. "Now, push the chair up there and put me to bed. Get on with it."

I lock her chair and stand in front of her. I fold up the footrest and put the stronger of her weak legs on the ground. Putting my arms around her neck, I pull her up and swing her around, pivoting her on her good leg. It isn't very gentle, but it's quick and the best I know how to do.

"You'd never make it in this business," she says as she sits down.

Two years ago at Thanksgiving, everyone was gathered outside my house to say good-bye. I was taking her out of the wheelchair and placing her in the car. I started to pivot her into the seat, when her head hit the doorway. She let go of my neck and dropped down. I hit the ground first, and she landed on my knees. I sat there holding my mother on my knee and started laughing. "Pick me up and stop laughing," she yelled. We sat there with Mother's legs all splayed out and her diaper resting on my knee. My sister and her husband came to the rescue and lifted her into the car, and I stayed there laughing like a naughty child. It was the last social event where we could convince Mother to join us—I'd like to think that I'm not the reason, but I'm afraid I might be at least partially to blame.

Now, two years later, Mother looks exhausted, but happy to be safely tucked in. She hasn't been out of the nursing home in two years, but at least she still trusts me to put her to bed.

—Judy Benowitz
Georgia

Illness is inevitable, but giving up is not. We Southern girls are strong, and we don't let a little thing like sickness interfere with our good times. When illness is more serious, when stroke or heart disease or cancer strikes us, our faith, families, and friends see us through.

Help in Time of Need

Although illness is something that Southern women face with strength, sometimes even the best of us are overwhelmed. Helping a friend, or asking for help yourself, in this difficult time is one of the true blessings of friendship.

- *In times of illness, people often tiptoe around a sick person as if she's a fragile little china doll. The person in that bed is the same friend you've always had, so treat her that way. Bring her all the latest gossip, a tape of her favorite comedy, or funny pictures of your grandchildren when you visit. False cheer won't help her, but sharing the things that the two of you genuinely love will.*

- *Asking for relief from pain is not giving up, and is certainly not weak. Numerous medical studies have shown that the body can better heal itself when it is not suffering from pain. Go ahead and ask for relief for yourself, or fight for your friend to get the pain treatment that she needs, so that you can get on with the difficult business of healing.*

- *If your friend wants to cry, let her cry. Getting out her emotions can give her some relief.*

- *Research how you can be a better helper for your friend. The library and the Internet are wonderful resources to learn about disease. Unless you are a doctor, of course, you cannot and should not be treating an ill friend, but you can learn about support groups in your area and nonmedical methods of helping your friend, such as diet and massage. If your friend doesn't want your help, of course, step back until she does. A Southern girl will know the line between being a helper and being a busybody and respect it.*

- *There comes a time in many illnesses when your friend realizes that the end is inevitable. Sometimes, all that you can do is hold her hand and pray.*

Saying Good-bye

Southerners know that death is a part of life, and though it is difficult, we face death with strength and courage. We're all afraid to die, but we know that our time will come. For Southerners with faith, death is not the end, but the beginning of a new phase of life. Those we leave behind may miss us, but there is still so much living to be done.

A God-Given Day

My mother had a bad heart for years. She needed bypass surgery, but her other health problems kept her from having it. She had had a brain tumor removed and was almost fully recovered from that when she fell at church one Sunday and ended up in the hospital for tests.

I stopped in at the hospital to see her on my way to work one Friday morning, and just on a whim decided to call in sick to work. I crawled up into the bed and stayed the day with her. Looking back now, I realize that it was no whim at all, but the work of God.

We spent the entire day laughing, talking, and just being to-gether. We shared one of the best days of my life. In the course of that hospital stay, the doctors determined that she was as healthy as she would ever be, and that it may be a good time for the heart surgery. She told me that day that she was going to go for it.

She asked, "What's the worst that can happen?" To which I replied, "Momma, you could die!" The next words I heard came from my mother's mouth, but they were the words of God, I'm sure. She said, "And go on to heaven? That wouldn't be so bad! I know that when I die, y'all will miss me, but you don't need me. My baby is grown and raising babies of her own. My life may or may not im-prove with the surgery, but it will do nothing but get worse without the surgery. I'm ready!" With that, I had full confidence that, regard-less of the outcome, she was doing the right thing!

Her surgery was the following Monday, and she blew us a kiss from the gurney as they took her out of her room. She never regained consciousness and died on Tuesday morning. Yes, good-bye was hard, but she had made it so much easier for me that day that I spent with her!

—Pat Miller
Alabama

Death is most difficult not for the dying—their suffer-ing has ended—but for the families and friends that are left behind. Southern funerals have always featured family and friends getting together, and huge quantities of food. We talk, we eat, and we even laugh. We gather together to cele-brate the life of the one who is gone; we lean on family and friends. Our rituals are a way of mourning those who have passed, but they are also a way of saying that we're still here, and that life will go on.

Helping Instant GRITS Grieve

GRITS stand by their friends in times of need. Sometimes, sadly, the friends who need our help are our children. Katie Couric, a Virginia GRITS, lost her dear husband. She advises parents to watch their children and to help them handle their grief in their own way. She says: "The other day my daughter Carrie was on her play telephone telling me, 'Mom, it's Daddy calling from heaven.' It was heartbreaking, but I wanted to explore it with her, so we started talking." Although her daughter was only a toddler, Ms. Couric recognized that she was saying something important in her own way. Adults, who are grieving themselves, need to remember that their children are also grieving, and they need to provide the explanations and comfort that they can in a way that the children can understand.

The Bull Dawg Fifty-Yard Line Will Never Be the Same

My dear husband, Lewis Grizzard, was a writer loved by men and women throughout the South, and when he passed away, I think a little bit of the South passed with him. Lewis's loyalty to his favorite team, the Georgia Bulldogs, was legendary. One of his last requests was to have his ashes sprinkled on the fifty-yard line of the Dawgs' football field.

Lewis died on the day before spring. It was the end of the season. We decided that it was time. Lewis's business partner, Steve, and I made the drive to Athens, Georgia. We picked up a six-pack somewhere along the way, and stopped to visit Lewis's father's grave in Snellville.

We arrived at Sanford Stadium, and all of the gates were locked. I suppose that we could have asked the University of Georgia to have a memorial service at the stadium, and with all the praise Lewis had given the school over the years, they would have obliged, but I wanted to keep it simple. So we scaled the wall.

When we ran out onto the field, we realized that none of the lines were painted. I didn't know what to do. Steve told me just to toss them; if anyone could find that line, Lewis could. As I tossed the ashes in the air, they turned golden in the light. Lewis had come to rest at his favorite place in the world, and I know that he's still cheering those Dawgs on from heaven.

—Dedra Grizzard, widow of the late Lewis Grizzard
Georgia

PEARL OF WISDOM

"With the death of every friend I love . . . a part of me has been buried . . . but their contribution to my being of happiness, strength, and understanding remains to sustain me in an altered world."—Helen Keller, Alabama

Time never heals the pain that we feel when a loved one has passed, but it can help to dull the hurt. I still have pain over the loss of those people I love in life, but every year, that pain grows less. When friends and family pass, it is important for us to mourn, but it is also important to move on with our lives. Those we love would not want for us to be consumed with grief. They would want for us to remember them fondly, to learn from their lives, and to move on with our own. Though they have passed, they are never gone from us as long as their memories and their love remain here.

WELL, I DECLARE

According to a recent poll by the Barna Research Group, while roughly seventy-one percent of Americans believe in hell, less than one-half of one percent believe that they are likely to end up there. Southerners are more likely to believe in heaven and hell than those in other regions of the country.

The Day I Stopped Worrying About Mama

The last three days had gone like clockwork. While we were making our funeral arrangements, several ladies from the church were cleaning the house. Every meal had been taken care of for us since Daddy died; sausage or ham and biscuits showed up in the morning, a roast and potatoes or maybe a sandwich platter at dinner, chicken and dumplings or fried chicken with greens and cornbread for supper, and plenty of iced tea. Someone even brought fried pies.

As the minister was preaching Daddy into heaven, he talked about Daddy's illness and how frail he had become. I nudged my sister Anna and whispered, "He didn't know Daddy very well, did he?" Frail was never a word used in the same sentence with Daddy, not even at the end. Roy Porter had always been a force to be reckoned with. He never went to church with us as long as I can remember, and after Anna and I grew up and moved out on our own, Mama went alone. Every Sunday morning, every Sunday evening, every

Wednesday; she never missed an opportunity. She always asked Daddy if he wanted to go, but I think she was secretly relieved that he didn't go because she was afraid he'd embarrass her. He wasn't one to keep his opinions to himself. And Mama, bless her heart, had to keep up appearances.

When we returned from the funeral, Mama busied us with heating up and setting out all the food that had arrived throughout the day. There was fried chicken casserole, a very large ham, greens, corn, cornbread, and every type of bean known to man, plus rolls, pecan pie, chess pie, a coconut cake, and two pound cakes. We laid everything out, and I remember thinking that my daddy had just died, and not only did I not want to eat, but I really didn't care if the locusts descending on the house had anything to eat either.

We slipped into the bedroom as people began to arrive. Mama needed to take a breath, and Anna and I thought she should change into something more comfortable. She stopped to check herself in the mirror when we heard a familiar voice outside the door. "I almost didn't recognize the place. You have no idea how hard they had to work to clean it up. Why, I was here just last week and this place looked neglected."

"They didn't need to work so hard," another voice responded. "You know Evelyn is always at church, but that scoundrel Roy hadn't set foot in church in almost twenty years!" Margaret and Camilla never had a nice thing to say about anybody who didn't happen to be in the room at the time. Anna and I looked at each other, but Mama's expression never changed. She put on more comfortable shoes and headed out.

Anna and I followed into the living room where aunts, uncles, cousins, and friends were eating and recalling their favorite stories about Daddy. Mama, Anna, and I sat down together and joined in the conversation.

Margaret and Camilla walked over, each wearing a weak grin, and probably wondering if we'd heard them through the bedroom door. "Evelyn, they did such a wonderful job on Roy," Margaret gushed, "He looked so natural."

Mama looked Margaret right in the eye. "The only way he would have looked natural was if he sat up and told y'all to go to hell."

It got really quiet really quick. Margaret and Camilla looked around and, finding no sympathetic faces, quietly left. As the door closed behind them, Mama shrugged. "Someone needed to do it."

The rest of the evening was filled with good memories of Daddy. We stayed up late and shared stories, some so familiar that I almost knew them by heart. As I was finally falling asleep, I was still missing Daddy, but I knew that Mama would be just fine.

—Carol Horton
Georgia

Making Peace

- We Southern girls like to keep a pleasant smile on our faces, even when faced with a serious illness of a loved one. It is often difficult for us to admit that someone we love may not make it. It's important, however, to tie up loose ends. If someone you love is seriously ill, take the time to make your apologies, and to show your love. Don't regret later what you left unfinished today.

- If you are a recent widow, don't be afraid to ask your friends and family for help. Those close to you will understand your need. Whether what you need is just a shoulder to cry on, or a serious crash course on finance and home maintenance, turn to those around you for support. Often, your friends and family want to help, but they don't know what they can do to assist you. Making them feel useful to you in your time of need is often helping them as much as it is helping you.

- When a loved one passes in the South, neighbors bring over enough food to feed an army. If you're in the South, don't let this tradition die out. If you are in another region of the country, take the time to spread this tradition. A family going through grief doesn't want to take the time to worry about what to make for dinner, and sometimes just the gesture, just knowing that others are standing by you in your time of need, helps to ease the pain. The best funeral food is something that is easy to store and to reheat, such as a casserole, but anything that you bring will be appreciated.

- The worst time for those left behind is often not right after the death, but in the weeks and months that follow. Take time to visit the bereaved after the cards and flowers have stopped coming, and offer to get the widow out of the house for a while. We often don't know what to say to someone in pain, but don't worry about the words. Your presence, your gesture of caring, is more important than finding the right thing to say.

Friendship Page

All Southern women value their friendships, but friendship means something different to each of us. Whether you're keeping this book for yourself or sharing it with a special friend in your life, take a few minutes to think about a friend who is important to you. Think about why she means so much to you, and how your lives have grown together. When you're done, share your feelings with your friend. Your love isn't something to keep hidden under a bushel; share it and let it shine!

MY FRIEND'S NAME:

WHERE WE MET:

MY FAVORITE THING ABOUT MY FRIEND:

SOMETHING BEAUTIFUL ABOUT MY FRIEND:

SOMETHING WE HAVE IN COMMON:

GOOD TIMES WE'VE SHARED:

TOUGH TIMES WHEN WE'VE BEEN THERE
FOR EACH OTHER:

THE MEN WE'VE BEEN THROUGH TOGETHER:

I'M LOOKING FORWARD TO:

Acknowledgments

Many thanks to Elizabeth Butler-Witter, not only a wonderful writer but a good friend. You made this book possible. Thanks to Bret Witter, for all his help, and your baby girl, Lydia Witter, for her inspiration. Thanks to my agent, Peter McGuigan; my editors, Trena Keating and Emily Haynes; and my publicist, Kathleen Schmidt, for all of your hard work on this project.